Unnecessary Talking:

The Montesano Stories

ALSO BY MIKE O'CONNOR

BOOKS OF POETRY AND TRANSLATION

The Rainshadow (1983)

The Basin: Life in a Chinese Province (1988)

Only a Friend Can Know: Poems and Translations on the Chinese Theme of Chih-yin (1997)

Setting Out: The Education of Li-li—a novel by Tung Nien (1998)

The Clouds Should Know Me by Now: Buddhist Poet-Monks of China (1998) (edited with Red Pine)

When I Find You Again, It Will Be in Mountains: Selected Poetry of Chia Tao (779-843) (2000)

Where the World Does Not Follow: Buddhist China in Picture and Poem (2002) (photography by Stephen R. Johnson)

When the Tiger Weeps (2004)

Icarus (2006)

ANTHOLOGY PUBLICATIONS

Working the Woods, Working the Sea: An Anthology of Northwest Writings (1986) (2007)

Paperwork: Contemporary Poems from the Job (1991)

Frontier Taiwan: An Anthology of Modern Chinese Poetry (2001)

The Wisdom Anthology of North American Buddhist Poetry (2005)

UNNECESSARY TALKING:

THE MONTESANO STORIES

For Shinto —
with affection —
in the Year of the Ox.

Mike O'Connor

Port Townsend

PLEASURE BOAT STUDIO: A LITERARY PRESS

MIKE O'CONNOR, a native of Washington State, is a poet, writer, and translator of Chinese literature. Beginning in the 1970s, he engaged in farming and forest work, followed by a journalism career in Asia that continued through 1995. He has published nine books of poetry and translation, and his recent long poem "Immortality" can be found on-line at *Narrative Magazine*. O'Connor is the recipient of a National Endowment for the Arts Fellowship in Literature, and he is an Honorary Fellow of Hong Kong Baptist University. He currently serves as publisher of Empty Bowl Press in Port Townsend.

ISBN 978-1-92935541-9
Library of Congress Control Number: 2008909909

"The Weld" first appeared in *Signs of Life*: *Contemporary Jewelry Art and Literature* (2007).

Frontispiece Photograph by Wallace R. Farquharson
Cover Art by Nina Noble
Editing Assistance by William Bridges, Jack Estes, and Chuck Thesing
Cover and Book Design by Nina Noble
Set in Sabon, designed by Jan Tschichold

PLEASURE BOAT STUDIO: A LITERARY PRESS
201 West 89 St., 6F
New York, NY 10024
Tel / Fax: 8888105308
www.pleasureboatstudio.com / pleasboat@nyc.rr.com

for my mother

Well well go & play till the light fades away
And then go home to bed
The little ones leaped & shouted & laugh'd
And all the hills echoed.

—William Blake, "Nurse's Song,"
from *Songs of Innocence*

TABLE OF CONTENTS

M ONTESANO, POPULATION 2,431 (excluding pets, visitors, and out-of-town prisoners) is the county seat of Grays Harbor, Washington State, a "bedroom community" of seaport Aberdeen, and home of the first tree farm.

The word Montesano derives from the Spanish and means "sane mountain," or "healthy mountain," but there are no mountains in or around Montesano, which is rather crazy.

1 THE FORT

W E BUILT IT from discarded wood from the torn-down Episco-pal Church on Sylvia Street. As the new Saint Mark's arose, we hauled the old one—board by nail-embedded board—away. Although many kids from around town joined in the construction, it was largely the Rachet brothers and I who built it, following my rudimentary design of 2 × 4 framing (an advancement from the two-sawhorse and sheet-of-plywood hideout design of my pre-school days) and Terry Rachet's wizard carpentry.

When building the first story, we made a special room, a dungeon, that had a small hinged door (the genius of Terry) and a lock, the idea being to capture an enemy and put him in there, and then, as a team, a firing squad, pee on him from a trap door (kudos again, Terry!) in the second floor. We also made wooden pallets to serve as beds for when we were wounded, attended (we imagined) by the Rachet boys' sisters, Emmy and Dottie, our Red Cross team. But the sisters rarely came around, owing to my mother warning they were too advanced for their ages.

Construction went well. Lots of kids in town dropped by to help us, as I said. Though we had to visit Doc Hopkins' several times for eightpenny nail punctures in our feet—we couldn't give up wearing tennis shoes, so had to take our tetanus shots and iodine swabbings without complaint—and though the three floors of the Fort went up pretty crooked, things got to the high-engineering point of our even pouring cement for a walkway, though the concrete never set.

We were building an addition under the pear tree when the Great Neighborhood Bean War broke out. Bean-Shooting War I should say. The Fort weathered many blistering bean attacks from Billy White's Catholic gang, but too many of our dozen defenders were exhibitionists and felt compelled to fall off the second story and die in dramatic fashion. One such capitulator, Ron Olsen, hit by a volley of lentils, threw himself off the third floor expecting a glorious attention-getting demise, but received for his effort a sprained ankle and, as he limped his way out of the yard, a merciless, stinging barrage of beans at close range.

Though we were able to just barely break the siege against the Fort, we were never able to capture anyone from Billy White's Catholic gang to put in the dungeon behind Terry's prison door. So after the war, which drained all the quarters I'd saved from my quarter-per-week allowance despite using—as the war and negotiations to end it dragged on—the cheaper split-pea instead of the higher-grade bean ammunition (the Rachet boys had no allowances, their father a logger), we had no recourse but to draw straws, and then threaten to lock the loser, Little Johnny, the younger Rachet, in the dungeon room and pee on him—an interesting idea to our credit we never took up.

That was just about the end of the active Fort period. The bean-covered yard around the Fort with a number of bent and discarded beanshooters on the grass were the only signs that a battle had taken place. There were no dead kids and the Fort itself hadn't been damaged by the warring, and soon spiders, banana slugs, and snails, which had taken refuge in the dank discarded lumber pile, moved back in.

A couple months later, with Father Frank's church now all but finished on the corner, a Seattle photojournalist, having coffee at the Bee Hive Koffee Shop, heard of the Fort. He came to our house and asked my mother if he could take a picture of the building with my sister and me on the top floor. The photographer got his picture (he didn't get the one of my mother which he had also asked for), but I really didn't feel comfortable with my sister up there with me; not that she wasn't a normal, okay sister (she was that and—to be magnanimous—more), but she hadn't helped build the Fort nor taken part in any way in the Great Neighborhood Bean-Shooting War. But it was peacetime now, and I guess in peacetime you have to bear a lot of things that you don't have to sit still for in time of war.

2 ANDY'S

Two blocks from our house and four blocks from school, just down the hill from the Spanish-style, adobe-roofed City Hall that also housed the library and fire station, was a little hangout for teenagers called Andy's. It had two pool tables and a jukebox, but wasn't a "greaser" place at all. Maybe certain things went on there I, as a fifth grader, didn't have the maturity to understand or even notice, or care to notice; but what was important was, thanks to Andy's, I was beginning to appreciate popular music and the fine art of playing pool.

The jukebox tune I most liked was Fats Domino's "Blueberry Hill" and the flip-side "I'm Walkin'." I also somehow got bowled over by an instrumental tune called "Theme from The Man with a Golden Arm." I had no idea why the man had a golden arm but I would have thought, if I had thought about it then, it was, perhaps, a baseball pitcher's arm.

Anyway, I played a lot of eight-ball pool there and got pretty good; good enough the high school guys would give me a little change when I beat them. In time, the only person who could regularly best me was the owner, Andy, and when he'd play me, with others gathered round to chuckle and watch, he'd play real serious. Even sweat a little. He didn't like losing to me in front of the customers; he didn't like losing to a fifth grader. But he was very gracious when he did and would give me a free Green River or a candy bar; or he might just say, "Okay. Now go ride your bike somewhere, Shark."

When school let out for the year, I always felt the incredible glory of being free again under June's warm, if cloudy, skies. I loved the last hours of school when you spent it all erasing everything you'd written in pencil in your textbooks and then got your deposit money back. (Too bad you used ink, Timmy.)

A bunch of us would head down to Andy's to listen to the juke-box and play a baseball pinball game that Andy had installed for us tenderfoots. It was a fun place, and I shot pool like a shark, as Andy would say, and it wasn't a hard or tough-guy place as our parents' talk over coffee might have suggested.

And even if it was "tougher" than, say, the Sunshine Ice Cream and Bakery just down the block, I figured a little toughness—whatever exactly that was in the context of Andy's—why, it might come in handy when I met up with any of Billy White's Catholic gang.

Also, Andy's wasn't occupying so much of my time that I wildly neglected other matters in my off-school hours: long rides on my bike to the Wynooche River Valley past the house of my girlfriend, Mary, who played the harp but whose father was a communist (that's another story); Little League baseball practice; swimming at Sylvia Lake State Park (on the kids' side; the other side of the lake had a float and the big kids swam there, and sometimes drowned there, too); even church on Sundays.

Andy's was, to my mind, an improvement over my gang's dependency on Mr. Bowen's Little Store near the high school for the penny candy we needed to carry us through late innings or the bean wars. After getting sick from sugar overdoses, I'd always swear I was never going back to the Little Store again. But in a day or two, with total amnesia, I'd be robbing my piggy bank—the pig had a cork plugging a hole in its belly—and heading off to the Little Store just three blocks away. When baseball cards became the craze, we chewed so many sheets of flat, pink powdery bubble gum trying to acquire the most famous players that our jaws would hurt all day.

The smaller Korean War card packets were better in this regard; they came without gum, just Korean War cards.

But in truth I didn't know, I don't think, what the teens were up to exactly at Andy's. I don't remember many people smoking there, just a couple of girls or guys sometimes outside by their customized cars. My allowance bank was even growing again from the pool games, now with the truce in the Bean-Shooting War, though I fed quite a bit of it back into pinball baseball.

"The Man with the Golden Arm" really triggered my interest in popular music, as I noted, and new tunes became favorites, like the one that began "Lonely rivers flow to the sea, to the sea." And I didn't even know I had a big sad heart until I'd heard that song. I must have been maturing faster than I thought, but for me growth was still measured by how much faster I could run than anyone else, excluding Patty Abendroth, a girl, which fortunately didn't count.

The high school girls, smelling like flowers in soft pretty sweaters sometimes would come up to me and ask if I would dance. And I would tell them, "If you put on 'The Man with the Golden Arm,' I'll give it a try."

But they usually just laughed and went back to their boyfriends or girlfriends. When Elvis Presley's "Heartbreak Hotel" appeared on the jukebox, it was just about the time one of my friend's sisters in junior high was teaching us how to bop. It was also about the time Billy Davidson and I were cooking toothpicks in pots of water with various fruit extracts to make flavored toothpicks to sell at the newsstand downtown on Saturdays. It was also around then that I was forbidden to frequent Andy's.

When my mother told me I was thus forbidden, I figured she was probably doing the bidding of Dad to some extent. The two of them worked well together. When parents operated separately—as any half-savvy kid will tell you—it left the door ajar for counterarguments as well as tantrums, fasts, and threats to run away to the woods.

My mother said she was sorry, but I'd find other, better ways to spend my time. "You've just got to stop going with your friends to Andy's," she explained without actually explaining.

"I can't play pool?"

"No. It's not the pool; you can play pool at Randy Hopkins', he's got a pool table."

"But Mom, that pool table is a miniature. It's not real."

So that was the end of my Andy's era. Not much later, someone told me there had appeared an article in the *Montesano Vidette* describing something that had happened at Andy's; and later, Andy's teen hangout changed into Judith's Yarn and Knitting Shop with strange tall bolts of fabric in all the windows. I didn't have to be a Mr. Wizard to know that Andy, of "Go ride your bike somewhere, Shark," wasn't running *that* business.

Whenever I rode past the new store on my bike, seeing what had become of the pool tables, the juke box, and pinball baseball—and even missing old Andy, who was rumored in jail, or at least had got himself run out of town to Aberdeen (a bigger, rougher town)—I felt a momentary sinking of my heart. But happily my gang and I, though we did miss Andy's, still had the promise of the whole wide summer vacation before us, and, putting cards on the spokes of our bike wheels (using clothespins) and colored plastic streamers on our handlebars, and lots of flavored toothpicks in our pockets, we rode off shirtless and joyful into the Chehalis-Wynooche countryside, oblivious to all controversy and loss.

3 MUCH ADO

I.

IT WAS A very big deal in the way of surprises when Duke Elmsworth, in Santa Claus suit, came to our house tipsy.

The honor usually befell us Christmas Eve. He'd do the Ho, Ho, Ho thing with my sister and me in the front room by the heavily tinseled Christmas tree, strung with bubbling tube lights—a tree my father had stealthily felled on Weyerhauser land somewhere near Satsop at dusk while my mother drove getaway car and we kids in the backseat sang "Holy Night"—and then Mr. Elmsworth, Santa, would swing through the door to the kitchen where my mom, dad, and a few friends were celebrating.

There'd be a big hurrah and someone shouting, "Santa Claus! Duke Santa Claus," from the glass-and-ice-cube clinking kitchen, and lots of Ho, Ho, Hos and other boisterous laughter, just as if Saint Nick and his elves were having a fete after sending off the last shipment of toy soldiers and candy canes to Grays Harbor. Once he was in the kitchen, we'd not see him the rest of the evening. He was as good as up the chimney.

I have to say, as much out of character as he was in that red suit, cap, and white beard on the eve of Christ's birth, he never quite masked from me the Duke Elmsworth I feared, the Lord of our hallowed halls, our grade school principal. I got scolded but never paddled by Duke Elmsworth, which recommends him, I dare say, as much as it commends my behavior. Everybody adult said he was a wonderful principal, patient, thoughtful, and lacking in sadism, which meant, I figured, he hadn't killed anyone yet. The power of his office, though—and his thick wooden paddle—could have easily tempted a lesser man into unbridled punitive fits resulting in more and more of us kids wearing books in our pants instead of carrying them in our satchels. ("Go ahead, Sir, right there on my *Dick and Jane Reader.*")

We kids knew Duke Elmsworth as a large bald-headed menace, roaming the grade school halls like a bear that never had to growl or show its claws. Even when he scolded you, for, say, squirting water at a classmate at the drinking fountain, he did it quietly. He was aware when he spoke to you that your heart would quit beating, so he didn't have to speak up to be heard over it.

"I'm only going to tell you once . . ."

That's how it would begin, even when, as in my case, he'd have to tell me more than once. Or, if his memory was keeping up with my offenses, he might say, "I'm not going to tell you again . . ."

After that, I'm sure the paddle came off the peg on his wall into play, but like learning where all the electric fences were strung on my grandmother's farm, I learned to stay within the field of safe conduct, which after all is exactly what Duke Elmsworth wanted; it's what the teachers wanted too, and the school board, for that matter, and the PTA. It's what Montesano wanted; it's what the whole country wanted; it was the educational program!

I'm sure without it, us kids would have transmogrified instantly into thugs, forming bicycle and tricycle gangs and burning down at least one of the churches on my block (there were so many in the neighborhood, no one would have missed one). We might have raided the candy store and started open bean-shooting wars outside the firehouse and library (actually we'd done that once until Mr. Jacobson, one of three permanent firemen, asked us to move our war-play down the block so in the event of a fire, the fire truck wouldn't make split-pea soup of us).

Perhaps, without the authority of the paddle, it might have triggered a kissing frenzy; they'd have to bring in the Aberdeen police to stop us. We might have gone to the movies on week nights, and we might have never gone back to school in September, but waited until the Gravenstein apples were all red, ripe, and eaten, and Indian summer had given way to October's rain-black skies.

Some of these things we might have done and some of these things I'm only saying to make a point, of a kind. But whatever way I might describe it, it came down to: Duke Elmsworth was the Law. ("Now children remember that the word 'principal' contains the word 'pal.'") Much scarier than Emperor Ming on "Flash Gordon," (who, come to think of it, we liked better than Flash or his girlfriend). BUT—and this needs to be made part of the record—he was not as scary as those hooded Ku Klux Klan posses, as seen by my sister and me in movies—Klansmen riding around at night in white sheets in the South, burning crosses and shouting unfriendly epithets at the people in their homes who used to be their loyal servants.

II.

In my second year of school, there was an incident that suggests something of the trepidation that pervaded our early school days. I almost confessed to a crime that I didn't even come close to committing, had never even conceived of as a thing of interest to do, just because of his, the principal's, apparent authority from some dark and higher entity than even the Shadow. "The Shadow knows"; but the dark and higher entity authorizing the principal knows better.

Duke Elmsworth came into our classroom and whispered to dear old Miss Whipple, also a bachelor, that he wanted all the girls in the class to go with her to another classroom; he would stay and have a little talk with us boys. This came while we were shouting out the names of colors on flash cards, shouting a little louder than normal because Miss Whipple was hard of hearing. "Brown! Yellow! Blue!"

The shouting died right there at "blue." The room fell as quiet as the inside of an abandoned boxcar on side-tracks along the Chehalis River, or the inside of an old tumble-down barn in which an owl has eaten all the doves, or the inside of the meat lockers on Main Street, or at the public library when strict Miss Webster was on duty. I swear you could've heard someone in the cloakroom sucking his thumb if someone had been in there doing it. (I wouldn't have minded being in there doing it rather than sitting trapped at my desk facing what looked to be bad music.)

Here is what the principal said: "One of you children used the wastebasket in the lavatory to go to the bathroom in, and it wasn't peeing. This was not a good thing to do; it was a bad thing."

His words cut the elevator cable that was holding my stomach on the ninth floor of the Bon Marché in Seattle. The fear of eternal damnation turned my face, if I could have seen it, as red as the one stoplight in Montesano when it's not green, when it's not yellow. My ears burned like fields of corn stalks set afire in fall. He wanted the boy (he assumed rightly, I figure, that it had to be a boy, though it would have been a good payback joke on us boys if it had been a girl, though I can't picture that!?) to confess.

The guilt I felt was so completely irrational (I would have felt no less terrified if I had done it) that I felt an impulse to confess that I *did* do it as some way to stem the tide of fear sweeping me out to a shark-infested sea, and part of that fear was that in some moment of confused non-repressed lavatory emergency, I'd actually done what I didn't actually do, namely substituted one white porcelain receptacle for a taller less-stable metal one. A confession held out hope of stopping the elevator on the third or fourth floor.

With this kind of neuron-surge, it's hard for a kid to find the rational handle. This was a lot scarier than the local theater's previews of

The Thing. This was even scarier than red-haired Terry Rachet, my neighbor, chasing me down the alley with a hatchet from his wood-shed, looking every bit like one of the devils in the Sunday school comic books, after I tried beating him up for kicking my dog.

Duke Elmsworth, in demanding the guilty kid stand up and come clean, didn't say anything like "It'll go easier on you if you do." Oh, no. I had the distinct impression that for whoever confessed to this indiscretion, things were not going to go easier at all. Just confessing would probably bring on a seizure like the kind Billy Watson had in the playground running between second and third base with the noon sun too hot for him, apparently, and he falling down and writhing in the base path while Eddie Philips, the third baseman, ran over and tagged him out "just to be sure it wasn't a trick," as he later explained to the school nurse.

So, Duke Elmsworth, who resembled a bear more than any other animal in Seattle's Woodland Zoo, walked on his hind legs slowly up and down the aisles. He stopped now and then to lean over a kid sweating in his desk, or chewing great bites out of his fingernails, or fighting back little second-grade tears. He looked into each kid's face, taking his time like a famous pianist who spends about a half hour to adjust his coattails, the piano seat, his delicate hands before slamming into Rachmaninov's Concerto for Piano and Orchestra in C minor, No. 2, Op. 18.

Duke Elmsworth was a he-bear waiting for a salmon to swim out from the shadows. He was the president of a serious and unhappy country declaring war on the Three Stooges ("Enough of their nonsense!"). He was Russia; he was the monthly enema for pinworms. He was liver at suppertime and a long year of rain. And I need not tell you the principal's face was not the Ho, Ho, Ho face of Santa Claus either; it was the red angry face of the Principal from God!

Finally, Duke Elmsworth spoke, "So, none of you did it?"

Every boy shook his head in unison like we were doing "The

Hokey-pokey" in the Little Gym without the music. "And no one saw anything?"

Again the heads went hokey-pokey. "Then could anyone please tell me how they think this might have happened?"

Hokey-pokey. We were getting into the rhythm of it now.

"No one has any idea at all?"

Hokey-pokey. Hokey-pokey.

"Don't you care for your school?"

Hokey-pokey. Hokey-pokey. "What?"

There was a moment of confusion as some heads went left and right while others began to nod forward. "Do you want me to get my paddle?"

Now we were in disarray, some heads nodding "yes" and others shaking "no." Duke Elmsworth was breaking us down!

I have more than once run through my imagination what it would have been like to be the kid who did the deed and confessed he did it, though no confession was ever forthcoming—but I agree with the principal, someone had to have done it. Either that or Duke Elmsworth had a bigger problem than just being principal.

Even as a partisan of outlaws like Billy the Kid and Jesse James, I must say the act was unsavory. But, on the other hand, who really knows the circumstances? And where was the lavatory monitor in all this? Shouldn't he be grilled for the act occurring on his watch? Or maybe that was the solution: someone was trying to frame the lavatory monitor. Perhaps the lavatory monitor had begun to over-step his authority, watching everyone so closely it was hard to even get the pee flowing during the short recess. But I can't even remember who our lavatory monitor was. It wasn't me; I was the kid who cleaned the erasers. Let's be clear about that.

But for whoever did it, how would they have ever lived it down if found out? If not found out, they might be having a good laugh right now, maybe thinking to get away with it again in a different school. I always brought home a report card that, among other things, was marked slanderously for Unnecessary Talking (a mere, if recurrent, misdemeanor to my mind), but how would the parents of the kid who filled the wastebasket feel when he brought home his report card that said: Gross and unnatural conduct; Johnny may need glasses. The Niagara of shame to the family and to the poor kid would force their immediate emigration to Elma.

If I had been the defense attorney for that kid, I'd definitely go with the insanity plea. My sister and her girlfriends sometimes laughed so hard at pajama parties they'd been known to wet their pants. And then would laugh even harder about the fact that they'd wet their pants. I could get one of them—not my sister—to testify about that kind of insanity.

Just before his leaving the room, Duke Elmsworth explained that the type of behavior exemplified by the wrongful use of the wastebasket was not only bad manners and a delinquent act, but that it posed certain health problems for all of us (which is how we kids viewed the principal). It also blemished the name of the school, teachers, and students alike. "Because no one apparently did it; you are all, in a sense, accessories."

"Accessories?" a few kids muttered.

"Yes, accessories." Then showing his own strain a little, he spelled "accessories." He did this slowly and with unneeded emphasis. "You are all a-c-c-e-s-s-o-r-i-e-s." He began to spell it again but broke off.

An empty-handed Duke Elmsworth left the room like a bear leaving a honeycomb that has comb but no honey, and all was as quiet as a tomb. You would have thought we might try laughing it off or at least look around at the probable suspects, but we just sat there like wooden pegs in a cribbage board until Miss Whipple came back trailed by a file of girls, and that should have been some kind of relief, normally, but in truth, we felt embarrassed and hoped they, the girls, didn't know what one of our kind had done.

III.

Several days later, we were being shown a film—a visual aid, they called it—in the same class, depicting the dropping of the atomic bomb on a Japanese city. Miss Whipple didn't want to show it, but the administration insisted. Of course, we'd watch anything; it was better than flash cards. The grainy film was the work of the Civil Defense people. It instructed us on what to do in the event the next bomb dropped our way instead of on the enemy. It wasn't fun.

After the showing, we were led in practicing getting under our wooden desks and covering our eyes because, they, the Civil Defense people, said the heat-flash from the bomb would blind us or peel us like a grape, even if it didn't land in the playground or on the school house roof. And Davy Lewis, a pretty good cut-up, barked out: "If they ever drop that thing on our school, whoever does it will have to go see Duke Elmsworth."

4 COMING TO A STATION NEAR YOU

I CAN'T EVEN now explain the mix-up. I can explain it, but I can't believe we were so mixed up. We had heard around town that television had arrived in Montesano. There had been talk before that it was coming, but the problem of getting reception had always been linked to having a station nearby. This was the source of the mix-up. We kids thought people meant by "station" a "gas station." "To get TV, you have to be close to a station," were the exact words of a mom. We were sure that meant a "gas station," though why we didn't think of "bus station," I can't say. We didn't think of "train station" either because the central one was in Aberdeen, and we didn't think of "a Station of the Cross" because—though we'd been taught something about such stations in Sunday school—we were too young to understand them.

Word spread among us of the imminent arrival. We even sang little ditties like "She'll be coming round the mountain, when she comes, when she comes," substituting "It'll" for "She'll"; and "Santa Claus is coming to town," with "Santa Claus" replaced by "Te-le-vision's coming to town." And coming that very day! to Pete Baylor and Jimmy Dockers' neighborhood; their neighborhood presumably being closer to a gas station.

A few of us went over to Pete's house after school. We tossed the football around until about four o'clock and then went in and sat in front of the big cabinet radio. It was a wooden radio set with a long horizontal glass tuner. We assumed, since we had never seen a television set, that the picture would appear where the glass for the tuner was. It certainly wasn't going to show up at our knees where the fabric-covered speaker was. There seemed to be plenty of room right above the numbered slash marks to receive a skinny picture. Hard to believe, I know, but we and Montesano were at the end of America; we were the last place to get new movies, new models of car, most news generally. What is more, we lived a long way from Battlecreek, Michigan. Any toy we'd send off for with cereal boxtops, such as baking soda-fueled submarines & frogmen, stamp books, and decoder rings, would take even longer than it seemed to take Roy Rogers, our talkative but much loved barber, to cut our hair. We'd send our coupons off with a little money in great anticipation, but by the time the prizes reached us, we'd grown several inches, gained several pounds, outgrown a pair of shoes, and changed eyeglasses. Fortunately, our brains didn't seem to change much, so (surprise! hurrah!) when the toy in question finally arrived, we may have forgotten when we'd sent for it, or even what it was, but we still knew exactly what to do with it, and would immediately send for something else.

At four-thirty, on the day our senses were forever going to be changed by the new medium, there in the shadow of the courthouse, we turned on the radio to "The Lone Ranger." Some five or six of us crowded into a sofa and a big armchair or seated ourselves on the viola case that belonged to Mrs. Baylor, a University of Washington graduate, who always kept a box of Graham Crackers, a loaf of Wonder Bread, and a big jar of Skippy Peanut Butter for us in the kitchen, and who, after work, drank beer like a dad from the bottle. We always said Mrs. Baylor had a way with kids, though we'd heard mothers say that with her college education and talent for the viola, she was wasting her life working at her husband's auto supply shop.

Anyway, there we were and about as excited as on the last day

27

of school. We were listening to, and staring intently at, the radio. The Lone Ranger, Tonto, and Silver were embroiled in one of their usual harrowing episodes, but all any of us could see were the numbers and slashes in the murky yellow light of the tuner. We waited and waited, only partly following the plot. We kept hoping that the reception problem would suddenly clear up and there in the living room of Pete Baylor's would be the Lone Ranger in his mask, Tonto in his feathered headband, and Silver, white as snow, chomping on his bit.

"Why isn't there a picture?"

"It'll come. Just hold your horses."

"Something is wrong."

"How can you say that? You don't even know what television is."

"Well, this ain't it."

Finally, it was "Hi Ho, Silver away" and the program was over. The program was over! We hadn't seen a thing we hadn't imagined in our radio-trained minds. We felt robbed; experiencing that emptiness a kid feels on opening a Christmas package with only a pair of socks nesting inside. If television planned to come to our town, it had just lost five or six viewers, is how we felt.

Our irritation subsided once back outdoors, dissipating in the brisk air, but it was getting too dark to resume tackle football, so again we felt disappointment.

We must still be too far from a gas station, is what we concluded, grabbing our bikes by their chilled handlebars, riding home in the last autumn light.

5 THE METAPHYSICAL COURTHOUSE

A T HALF PAST five in the afternoon in early fall when dusk was stealing upon our town, we'd hear the clock tower, feel its iron-jolt in our hearts, telling us with just one stroke to cease our play. It was loud, too, there by the very ramparts of the courthouse—we could not disobey it.

"Clang! Go home. Leave off your play," was the gist of it.

Our playing field wasn't big, level, or shaped right for tackle football, but the grass field, owned and mowed by the county, was green, centrally located and, as a bonus, largely free of dog doo, the bane of both tackled and tackler.

Our field was just across the lane from the county jail that was at the back of the huge sandstone-faced courthouse. The two-story jail was a nondescript block of concrete like a bunker, and given the architecturally imposing nature of the front of the courthouse, the jail reminded us of the backside of a tom turkey.

The courthouse had a copper-dome with a cupola on top, and below the cupola on all four sides, clock faces lit up in the night like moons. Of course, considering the Roman style of the courthouse, and all those clock faces, the clock tower had to ring out the hours and strike a reminder bell every half hour. It had to do something, being at the epicenter of county political power with so many busy and well-dressed people coming and going through its doors each weekday.

In truth, the clock tower rang through all the days of my childhood, through all my minutes of study and hours of play, through the long hard rains of Grays Harbor and the days of holy sunshine and emerald lawns. It was like a heart beat: always working but seemingly unnoticed, except by us, and especially at the black and fatal hour of half past five.

We could easily have gone on skirmishing way after dark, although weakened by hunger, and with every play from scrimmage, increasingly giggly; but everyone in Montesano ate supper roughly between six and six-thirty. (I should say, "approximately"; they didn't eat, as far as I know, "roughly.") And, in Montesano, and I presume the world, supper—a great thing in itself—meant nuisances: changing clothes, washing hands, fingernails, and face, and most difficult of all, calming down.

"Calm down now." Which was exactly what I'd tell Carolina, my cocker spaniel, after I had arrested her flight to devour Mayor Ingham's old cat that lived with the Inghams across the street from us. "Calm down, Carolina." I'd say as the poor dog shook and frothed while I held her back by her ears.

"Calm down, Mike," my mother would say, as—suddenly done with the washroom—I'd feel a terrific stab of hunger and go skidding into the dining room rattling the place settings and raising my father's eyebrows and my sister's scorn.

"Settle down now," my father would say, and shortly thereafter my sister would piously intone grace.

Thanks to television finally arriving to our town, if supper was perchance delayed, it might mean a quick peek at Flash Gordon and Emperor Ming on one of our two Magnavox-TV channels in a never-ending series of fabulous worlds bridged by spark-showering rocket ships.

After everyone began eating, passing the various dishes around the table like an infield whipping the ball around the horn after a quick out, my mother sometimes protested that she wasn't a very good cook, but I always liked just about everything: from creamed clams to waffles to steak and potatoes. And there was a predictability about the menu I liked too: the same meals appeared not so far apart, hence a kid could usually know what was in the dugout and what was on deck.

Meat and potatoes, a staple, were always ahead of the other dishes in appearances, and a big stew—my least favorite—landed squarely on every other Sunday. Fudge, ah, no one makes fudge like my mother used to make. It wasn't exactly a meal, although both my sister and I—eating it fresh from the oven after previously and dutifully licking the spoons and bowl—would have gladly stretched it into one had not my mother kept in mind our dental records. By the way, I never heard my father complain about my mother's cooking, though we did eat quite frequently at the Bee Hive Koffee Shop. He wasn't, in other words, averse to taking Mom and us out to eat whenever possible; you could say he rather encouraged it.

Once, when my mother was off with other mothers on a Christmas shopping trip to North Gate in Seattle, my father cooked in her place. I had assumed we were going to eat at the Bee Hive Koffee Shop, where my favorite food was a hot roast beef sandwich and mashed potatoes smothered in gravy. But no, Dad actually put on Mom's flowered apron, which seemed as incongruous as me twirling my sister's rubber-tipped marching baton. And it was also strange just my mother not being there in the kitchen that seemed so much hers, like when the drummer of our school band was sick and we practiced without percussion. Yet Dad, amid bubbling pots and steamed-up kitchen windows, had cooked some meat and lumpy mashed potatoes, which looked okay. But ugh! The meat turned out to be liver, and I ate some and hid the rest in my hill of potatoes, which were tasty, but now I couldn't eat them because the hill of them was employed to hide the liver. With Mom there, we would never have had the liver in the first place, but if we had she would have cooked us something else once I protested—a couple times.

Dad, though, offered no apologies, and I suspected no protest was going to make him don the apron again. My sister, who just *loved* my dad, was snapping down the liver like it was deep-fried Westport razor clams, and talking to Dad about the A she got on her latest English paper on Filial Responsibility of Kids, or something. So finally Dad reaches over to my plate with his fork and delicately exposes the pieces of liver hidden in my scoop of mashed potatoes (which was like that movie where the runaways hide in a haystack and the farmer uses his pitchfork to flush them out), and Dad gives me a knowing look, retracts his fork, and goes on eating.

I ate each liver piece like it was a big vitamin pill, trying not to chew it more than enough to get it down the ole tube. Well, at last I got to eat the mashed potatoes and cleaned up my plate like—as they say—"a good little boy" in expectation of dessert.

"Sorry, kids, no dessert tonight," Dad announced.

Before plummeting into despair, I had the thought that this situation was probably not unlike the time when Dad (as I had heard it) announced a twenty-mile hike to his all-colored troops at Fort Lewis during the war. The troops finally come to the end of their march and collapse on the Nisqually Scotch broom prairie. "We're pooped. Where's the bus?" and Dad tells them, "No bus back to the barracks, men. It's part of the program."

But let me say, that was all the stricter Dad ever got. Most of the time, he was only a minor obstruction to my childhood, and later I would be grateful to him for letting me sip a little of his beer and for letting me drive, without a license, his old green pickup to the dump with him.

II

But back to that clock tower! If Cinderella had lived in Montesano, the fancy ball she went to would have ended at half past five rather than midnight. (If Cinderella had lived in Montesano, we'd have put her on the top of our Fort!)

From the alley behind my house I could always see the eastern face straight on; from Jimmy Dockers', the northern one—it was so close to his house in fact, Jimmy once took it for the moon in his upstairs window where his model airplanes hung by strings from the ceiling.

From downtown looking uphill, the south face and pillared entrance appeared stately and governmental, and from Billy Raymond's, you could look down from the highest hill in town on the north face, too. Where was I when I was on the west side of town? I don't remember seeing the clock from there. Maybe from Tommy Thomas's house, the biggest kid in our class, whose dad was a state patrolman, and whose name was the same as his son, Tommy Thomas.

You could see the clock tower from practically anywhere in town. You actually could go all the way across the first bridge over the Chehalis River floodplain, past Vancouver Door, which made doors and sponsored my Little League baseball team, on past the burning giant wigwam that was the wood-waste furnace of the plywood mill which you could see aglow through the night—its sparks dancing into the stars—past the marshes where we built makeshift rafts but couldn't get them to go because the reeds, filled with red-winged blackbirds, were too high and the swamp water, thick with duckweed, too low, and we didn't dare to venture out to higher water and get caught in the powerful main current of the river, carried off to Aberdeen to feed a saw mill, or be Shanghaied to Hong Kong, or Hong Konged to Shanghai, or reach the ocean without provisions and not having told our parents where we were going or when we'd be back.

You could go across the bridge, as I was saying, and still see the southern face of the courthouse clock on the hill above town. We'd sometimes stand on our rafts imagining that we were moving, floating somewhere with our poles stuck in the mud and gaze back toward the courthouse. We weren't consciously proud of it or anything, but it was pleasant to observe its augustness, to salute its quiet columned dominion from that distance set off by the green forested hills behind it, familiar still, but giving old anchorage and fresh perspective to our town and to our lives.

If I were to imagine myself being that courthouse with that clock tower, with eyes and brain and everything, I'd find it quite amusing observing all the kids below revolving through the day—to school, to noisy playgrounds, to homes and little backyards with sandboxes or croquet sets; riding streamered bicycles, red scooters, zipping about on roller skates, dragging wagons flanked by dogs, flying down hills in soapbox carts with the wheels coming off, climbing without permission in a neighbor's fruit tree, clambering in and out of parents' cars and the accordion doors of school buses, skipping rope, blowing bubbles, jumping hopscotch, shooting marbles, teeter-tottering, tossing jacks, building forts, playing guns, hide and seeking, and even going solemnly to the dentist's, the doctor's, the barber's or the library . . . leaving everything be itself out there in our county seat town above the banks of the old Chehalis River, letting everything stir around me, even welcoming the rain-colored clouds rolling in from the ocean and the strong ocean winds pitching in the swaying firs and poplars.

This would be my old stone-edifice way, passive, benign, only reminding everyone with my bells of the hour and the half hour, harmless until half past five. Only then would I regretfully inflict upon the happy children of the town that single bell to toll them off the play fields, to toll them home. It would be inevitable, institutional and programmed, not personal, but nonetheless written, if not in the stars, then in the American customs of a newly settled coastal people.

But if I was really the courthouse, I'm sure I'd find a way to skip, subvert the striking of that bell at half past five; I'd hold back the clapper defiantly until at least six. I'd give all the kids a dispensation, yes, like a pope, and the kids would all look up to me in the surprise of my silence, bow their heads and commence playing another half hour or until their wild engines sputtered and ran completely out of gas. At least they would thank me for this until it all became accepted, taken for granted, like water from the kitchen tap. But I wouldn't care. Not a whit. Being taken for granted is exactly what a true benefactor is looking for. It's like being a good parent.

III.

We played mostly tackle or flag football (we all hated touch because it made plays into the scrimmage line pointless) on that grass field—Jimmy Dockers, Pete Baylor, Billy Raymond, Randy Hopkins, and many others. While we played, an inmate or two would watch us sometimes from behind one of the barred windows just across the tree-lined lane opposite our field. Sometimes a prisoner would wave, call out something to us, and on occasion we went and stood under his window—autumn leaves floating down around us—and talked to him. There was something of that feeling when you go to see a person in the hospital—you're polite but uneasy and don't want to hurt the feelings of the person suffering, but don't want, on the other hand, to stick around too long and catch a disease.

"You boys are pretty darn good."

"We want to play on the high school team some day."

"Oh, I'm sure you will."

"Why are you in jail?"

"Oh, I got in a little trouble, but I don't have to stay long."

"Did you rob a bank?"

"No, no. Nothing like that. You boys wouldn't be interested."

"Did you kill someone?"

"Oh, no [laughter], I just got in a little fight."

"Did you win?"

"Yeah, sort of."

"How long do you have to stay?"

"Just a couple more weeks."

"Do they feed you any good in there? Can you read books and comics? Do you have a radio?"

"Oh, yeah, I eat real well and everything. It's not for long like I said. It was just a little scuffle, you know."

This was often the case— "just a little something or other." It was always hard to make out who we were talking to because the bars on the window were so narrowly spaced that you couldn't squeeze a cake with a knife in it through if you wanted to (we weren't sure we wanted to); and the bars masked parts of every jailbird's face, though when they talked to us, they usually gripped the bars with their hands, and we could always tell from their hands that they weren't piano players.

In the couple of years that this went on during football season, it always seemed we were talking to vaguely the same guy, though it wasn't always so. For example, one jailbird with very bad teeth told us he'd already killed sixty people. He also suggested we should play in the lane closer to his cell window so he could watch the cars run over us.

There was another inmate, a smoker, who said he hadn't done anything.

"Then why are you in jail?"

"I'll tell you why," he said. "Because it's a goddamn mistake."

"What did they say you did?"

"That doesn't matter."

"For swearing?"

"They don't put you in jail for swearing, son."

"Why did they say you did it?"

"Hey, if I knew that I wouldn't be in here."

"Did you kill someone?"

"I'd like to."

One prisoner really put us on. "What are you in for?" (We were learning the jargon.)

"I robbed a stage coach."

"A stage coach?!"

"Yep, and I almost got away but the Sheriff shot the legs out from under my horse."

"Was that out West? We'd all like to go out West and be cowboys."

"Well, boys, if you went any further west you'd be in the goddamn ocean."

At first the swearing startled us; it wouldn't have startled Billy White and his Catholic Gang. But after a while we grew comfortable with it; and then I made the mistake of trying some of it at home.

"Where did you hear that, Mike?"

"What, Mom?"

"That word you just said."

"What word?"

"You just said g-o-d-d-a-m-n."

"I did?"

"Yes you did, little man." ("Little man" was not good. "Son" was better.)

"I guess it just slipped out."

"Yes it did, but where did you hear it."

"Billy White," I lied.

"That boy. He needs to have his mouth washed out with soap."

"Can you do that to another mother's kid?"

"Of course not, but I can wash out yours."

I knew all the exhortations against lying, but each year it got harder to refrain from it, as I became a more complex personality with increasingly complex relationships, objectives, subterfuges, schemes, and responsibilities. But this lie I considered a white one (no pun intended) because I didn't care if Billy White caught a little slander if it meant protecting our access to jailbirds.

Often we'd hear the striking of the courthouse clock, hoping, but knowing better, that it was only half past four. Soon after, just in case we were trying an end-run around time and space, in other words, reality, Jimmy's mom, a kind of back-up-bell designate, from their nearby house, called Jimmy to supper, and we'd all say good-bye to the prisoner of the day, and he'd say, "See you boys tomorrow."

Then we'd say, "For your sake, we hope you don't."

We'd cross back over to the field, pick up our bikes from the grass (we had a prejudice against kickstands; they took too much time to set up and usually our bikes got knocked over by a wild pass or kickoff) and ride like furies home.

Billy Raymond wondered once why there never were girls in the jail, just men. I told him girls didn't do crime; they just let their men do it. Pete Baylor thought that they did have girls in jail, that they sometimes drove getaway cars for their men who sometimes slapped them around and called them dolls. (Pete wanted to be a policeman.) Later, after their arrest, Pete continued, the women went to a special place where they couldn't be seen. "That would be punishment enough for girls," he said.

We always kept a certain aloofness from whoever was in the windowed cell (they changed jailbirds quite frequently), but also we were quite civil to, and curious about, them. I don't think any of us discussed these encounters with our parents; it just wouldn't have sounded right. "Hey, Mom, we had a swell talk with a man in jail today. He said he beat up a guy in a bar but was very sorry about it. He also said Jimmy's got what it takes to be a high school quarterback."

Or: "Home already, son?" my Dad might say. "Did you have a good time at school? Anything interesting over at the county jail?"

Curiously, we often received more convincing moral instruction from certain jailbirds than we did from either Sunday school or our parents. One prisoner for example, an older man, said he was in the slammer for getting drunk again.

"My whole life," he told us, "has been one long drunk. And once I was pretty good in school, too. But after the war, I couldn't get a decent job. So I just decided to drink instead of work, though I tried to do both for a time."

"Gee, that's terrible," one of us said.

"Yeah, it stinks don't it? But let me say something to you kids: I'm sure you're thinking it's all gravy, this world for you now, but you have to keep your eye on the ball, and I ain't talkin' football or baseball neither. I tell you this because otherwise when trouble starts lookin' for you, if you ain't paying attention, you're never gonna see what hits you."

This was chilling, and the several of us standing beneath the jailbird's window were mute. Then the courthouse clock struck and, for once, we eagerly dispersed.

VI.

After school in the crisp October air with the pleasant smell of burning leaves and rotting apples, there'd almost always be someone behind the bars of those county jail windows watching us kids free as birds whooping and shouting and tossing a football up and down in our exuberant world. As the jailbird said, it was all gravy.

The men in the cell windows bore some resemblance to out-of-work loggers we knew or mill hands who we might pass on our bikes as they went in and out of the noisy downtown neon-lit taverns late afternoons on the south side of the main highway, a highway that went straight through Montesano like an arrow under the lone wind-swung stoplight in the dead center of town. They weren't the shop people we saw regularly, nor were they like our dads, who were mostly professionals—Randy's was our doctor, Billy's was the editor of the newspaper, my dad was with the Department of Agriculture, and Jimmy's was a big car dealer, though I had once heard the word "crook" associated with that profession, though not necessarily with Jimmy's dad.

Clearly the jailbirds, over several seasons, made a lasting impression on us, but it wasn't the same as we got from the villains in movies, tough killer crook types. No, our jailbirds were quiet, sadder men who lived in our town, or at least county, somewhere.

"What do you mean they live in our town?" said Timmy.

"Where do you think they live?" said Billy.

"I've never seen them in our town, except in jail."

"You just didn't recognize them in normal work clothes."

"It's like communists," I explained. "They look just like any other citizen until you see them in their secret circumstances."

The prisoners in those gray windows watching us outside playing must have—at some time or other in their uneventful days—remembered or thought some about when they were young and out there on a field just like ours, and though they were old enough to know that they could never be out there the way we were now, they might find a way to keep from, with luck, in the unpredictable future, being in there where they were presently, again.

Or maybe not. Maybe, in their minds, it was already too late to reform unless they moved far away beyond the sandstone and shadows of the courthouse, to where they never would run out of cascara trees to peel, peas to pick, or rutabagas to dig. This is speculation, but I'm trying to get at something and to avoid saying not everything was perfect in Montesano, which of course was true I sensed in some social way, but which knowledge I was then reluctant to admit into the sunnier realms of my intellect. Because most of the time things were close enough to perfect in Montesano and I didn't want to jinx that. But those men in jail planted a seed of doubt, for sure. Maybe Montesano was moving along fine, but I started to suspect that something in the world at large wasn't. And who could be happy thinking too much about that?

And as a kid, I didn't. In say ten minutes from leaving the scene of our play, and back home watching "Flash Gordon Conquers the Universe," serial chapter XI on TV, starting to salivate a little from the cooking odors coming from Mom's kitchen, I didn't even recall a single jailbird or even for that matter who'd won our tackle game. And yet . . . and yet I had begun to sense that something was not fair in the world, something hard to fathom, unnerving (maybe related to that jailbird's "when trouble comes looking for you"), and at some undetermined point in the colorful, vibrant flow of life, whatever it is or is called, it comes along and breaks your heart.

Like half past five.

6 THE NAME'S THE SAME

I.

THERE WAS THE dentist office and then there was the barbershop; the latter painful in a different way than the dentist office, but painful. Don't get me wrong; we—my gang of friends—liked the barber. He was an older man who had—as my mother often said—very nice manners, but *we* liked him especially because of his name.

The first time my mother took me there, I lost most of my anxiety because of that name. It was also why we were loyal to him, even when younger and faster barbers came to town. The whole barbershop experience could have been almost pleasant if it wasn't for the waiting. Waiting to get in the chair and waiting to get out. The dentist was nice too, once he'd put away his big rumbling drill, and he was much younger, and for better or worse, we knew every blonde hair in his nose.

The barber's name was Roy Rogers.

We'd been fooled once by our class cut-up, Davy Lewis, into thinking Davy's dad, Joe, was the Joe Lewis who had been so famous on the radio's Pabst Blue Ribbon fights. I was listening to one fight with Dad, being held in Aberdeen, that must have come at the very end of the real Joe Lewis's career or it surely wouldn't have been happening in Aberdeen at all because anything of national sports significance happened far from Montesano. I listened to the whole fight thinking it was Davy's dad who got knocked out in the seventh round.

As I said, we all thought Joe Lewis—meaning Davy Lewis's dad, who in reality was a county agent—was the actual Joe Lewis, the fighter, and how could we know otherwise since we rarely saw him and had never seen the real Joe Lewis.

Though the barber's name was Roy Rogers, his wife's name was Gertrude, not Dale, and when we finally did get TV, we saw a show called *The Name's the Same,* and we decided to ask Roy Rogers, our barber, not the cowboy, if he'd be on it.

The next time I was sent for a haircut, I was determined to ask him. As usual, the barbershop was filled with adults, and because Roy Rogers was the slowest barber in the world, I knew I'd be a hostage until suppertime. There was a big pendulum clock against the wall that ticked loud enough to be in our school band, and it seemed to take pleasure in ticking away any hope I might have had of getting over to Jimmy Docker's place before dark for basketball.

The men in the room, though, seemed content to be there, reading newspapers, talking to Roy Rogers, and chatting among themselves. Because there were lots of workingmen waiting for haircuts, Roy Rogers kept a big brass spittoon for the tobacco and snuff-chewing elements. Every so often, one of the men got up from his newspaper or talk and moseyed over to the cuspidor and spat. I watched them do this, but I tried to avoid looking into the spittoon itself—shiny brass on the outside and swimming with old spit and cigarette butts inside.

Naturally, I had to try out the spittoon myself; I couldn't just sit there for years watching all the men use it without being influenced. I put down my *Reader's Digest* and ambled over to the cuspidor and spat. I was known in the neighborhood as having a fairly neat spit on the ball field, so I felt confident I could stand a few steps from the target and hit it. I was spitting, however, a pretty thin wad of saliva compared to the tobacco torrents of the men, and my spit only reached the outside brass.

"Hey, boy, what kinda tobacco you chewing?" and the whole

43

room—and I think the clock too—broke into laughter.

Rebuffed, I spit again even harder, and I overshot the spittoon and hit someone's long coat on the wall above. You could say I was getting spitting mad, so I went to right over that brass cuspidor and spit directly into it. "There," I said.

"There, indeed," said one of the men. "This kid's a spitfire. Ha, ha, ha!"

"Yeah," said the man whose coat I'd hit. "I'm going to send his mama a laundry bill. Ha, ha."

Roy Rogers put down his clippers and came over to the spittoon and, using a paper towel, cleaned off the spit from the coat. "Roy, don't worry about that," said the owner of the coat. "What you need to do is get the kids their own spittoon." Everyone laughed.

"Maybe the kids need a cartoon spittoon," said another man brightly, but no one but the man who said it laughed.

II.

In addition to the unsavory spittoon, there was, of course, a lot of clipped hair on the floor of the shop. But after each customer got his ears lowered, Roy Rogers carefully and, of course, slowly swept up the floor, talking all the while as he did. For a barbershop, Roy Rogers' shop was mostly clean and comfortable, and warm in winter; but the waiting was excruciating and cancelled out the positive amenities.

On that particular day, I was especially eager to get into the barber chair, not because I thought there was any chance of getting out of it before dark, but because I wanted to ask Roy Rogers about *The Name's the Same*. Finally my turn came. I was just about the last customer before closing and I was darn tired of watching the clock, reading the *Digest*, and thumbing through old copies of *Life* magazines.

"Okay, Mike. You're up."

While the man who just preceded me was digging out his leather wallet and simultaneously working to get an arm poked through a sleeve of a red hunting jacket, I climbed into the big chair with the metal footrest and settled in. It reminded me of being on a throne, but in my case, my crown was about to be diminished.

"So long, Fred," Roy Rogers said to the man going out the door. The door had a bell; and the man said, "Good-bye, Roy." Jingle-jingle.

After sweeping up that customer's hair (former hair?), Roy Rogers sailed a big sheet over my body and pinned a paper collar around my neck. He dug his clippers out of a drawer and said, "Crewcut, right?"

"A G.I. crewcut, please."

While he cut my hair, I waited for an opportunity to ask him about the game show, but Roy Rogers had plenty of things he wanted to ask me about first: my dad, my mom, even my sister. As he worked on me, he asked how I was doing in school; did I like my teachers; was I playing ball (not this afternoon, Sir); had I seen the new house being built over on Spruce Street (Seen it? We'd been playing guns there for six months). Then Roy Rogers told me that when he was a kid a million years ago they had to have their haircuts at home because the town he grew up in was even smaller than Montesano and wasn't almost a town, except for a train depot, a church, a supply store, and a one-room school house.

"Mr. Rogers, may I ask you a question?"

I was sitting still as stone in the chair but using my hands under the sheet to occasionally knock the freshly cut hair, amassing on the sheet, onto the floor, while Roy Rogers wriggled his clippers at the back of my head.

"Why certainly," he said, tilting my head a little forward and down while he went after some more hair in the back.

"Would you like to be on *The Name's the Same*, Sir?'

"Pardon?"

"Would you like to be a contestant on that new television show *The Name's the Same?*"

"Oh, I think I've heard about that one," he said.

"Well?"

"Well what?"

"Well, would you like to be on that show? They fly you to a TV station and give you a hotel to sleep and eat in and you can win some big prizes."

"I don't think I want to be on that show. But thank you for asking me."

Then he handed me a mirror so I could see my head reflected from the wide mirror behind me.

"Does that look all right?"

I looked and saw what I only got to see at the barbershop. Is that my head? I thought it looked pretty strange in the mirror that way: a shape like a coconut and without much more hair than a coconut either. I handed back the mirror to Roy Rogers.

"But why don't you want to be on the show? Your name is Roy Rogers, isn't it?"

"It sure is," said Roy Rogers, the slowest barber in the West.

"You know what that means, don't you?"

He put the mirror down and picked up a brush with soft white bristles and powder and began whipping it around my shoulders and the back of my neck.

"Oh, I know what the name means. And I'll tell you a little secret. I've had the name longer than the other Roy Rogers."

Wow. I had to think about that because I hadn't thought about it before. "I guess he should be on the show then, not you."

"Well, but he's made the name famous. Everybody knows who he is. Only people in Montesano know who I am."

"What about the free plane tickets and the prizes?"

"Oh, that flying in airplanes is a lot of bother, don't you know? Mrs.

Rogers and I are getting a little too old for that kind of thing."

"And the prizes?"

"Why, Mike, to be perfectly honest with you, Gertrude and I have just about everything we need already."

"Everything?'

"In a manner of speaking."

Boy, this was new territory for me.

"Mr. Rogers?"

"Yes, Mike?"

"Can you tell me where Jimmy Stewart's office is located?"

"Oh, you mean the new lawyer in town?"

"Yes, Sir, that would be him."

7 TONSILLECTOMY BY ALIENS

IT WAS WINTER and I was little. With only an inkling of why, one morning I was taken to the place of my birth: Saint Joseph Hospital in Aberdeen.

"You're going to have your tonsils taken out," my mother said.

"Is this going to take very long?"

"Not particularly, and once they're removed you won't be getting so many sore throats."

"And that's why were driving to Aberdeen?"

"You're going to feel much better after it's over."

The hospital proved a pretty grim affair, but that grimness worked wonders as an incentive to stay healthy and out of it. Being as I was Episcopalian, not Catholic, the nuns who worked there startled me with their costumes. The younger nuns still had nice faces, but the older nuns looked like theirs had been pinched too long in their headwear. There were several of us kids penned up in iron-railed beds waiting to be slaughtered. The nurse-nuns were constantly wheeling kids in and out of the room, to and from surgery. One kid strapped to a cart was wheeled away while he went on reading a comic book. This gave me hope. But when they wheeled the kid back a little later, he looked dead and his comic book was gone.

Did I mention the smell of ether and disinfectant? Well, it was as pronounced as the methane smell in my farm grandmother's chicken house. The light in the room wasn't so good either. It was basement light, or the cold light in the Ford dealer's garage under a car where mechanics slide around on their backs on small-wheeled dollies tinkering with flat-8 engines.

Finally my turn came. They strapped me on the four-wheeled cart and pushed me down the hall to the operating room. The ride wasn't bad at all, but when they boomed me through the swinging doors of surgery, I swear I thought I was being loaded onto a spaceship. There were all kinds of machines and instruments in that room and everyone was dressed and masked in white. There were no nuns, judging from the costumes, and I was put directly under bright lights. Then a rubber mask was fitted over my face, and I was instructed to count slowly backwards from one hundred. I was pretty sure it was a spaceship now, as I counted down to blast-off.

At this point I was thinking how lucky I was that I had so much experience of space from watching movies. There was an outside chance I'd be able to communicate with whomever I bumped into. They had asked me to start counting down from one hundred, so I figured it was going to be a while before we reached lift-off. I also was glad they hadn't asked me to count down from anything higher because that was the top limit of my numbers.

100, 99, 98, 97, 96 and then I woke up in my flimsy open-backed hospital gown and returned to my pen in the ward with the other kids, who were either on their way into space or who had recently returned. Soon, a young nun-nurse came by and offered me a small dish of ice cream. I started to thank her, but she put her hand up and said, don't talk yet. I tried to thank her again, but there was no voice in my throat, just a terrible aching. What had the aliens done to me?

"You'll be able to talk in a little while, but just now, eat your ice cream and rest."

Then a nun in a big habit, one of those with the older, pinched faces, swept over to my pen in her robes and smiled and mumbled a prayer over me. I was still pretty hazy in my head from the etherized space journey to catch all of it, but it sounded like she was telling God to be good to me because I'd been badly used by the hospital.

I don't know how many hours I stayed in the hospital, but I do recall when my mom and dad finally got around to taking me out of there, I was fairly irked at them both. They'd probably been off shopping at the big department store—the one with the soda fountain and the toys on the third floor—or at the movie house where *The Shaggy Dog* was playing, while their son was being tampered with across town. They were probably having lots of fun with their throats, eating popcorn and hot dogs, and shouting happily.

On the way home, it began snowing and I became excited thinking about snowball fights and sledding. But once home, I was bundled off to my room and put to bed. I was told I couldn't get up until the next day and couldn't go outside for at least three days. Adding insult to injury, my mom also told me I couldn't suck my thumb any more or I'd have to go back to the hospital for another operation.

"Sucking your thumb will aggravate your tonsils."

"But Mom, I thought they took my tonsils out."

8 THE WELD

For us boys spring's arrival always meant marbles, yo-yos, and especially soapbox carts. Every year the wheels on our carts got bigger—baby carriage wheels gave way to wagon wheels, and wagon wheels to old bicycle tires. Two 2 x 4s for axels, one long plank for the undercarriage, and a peach crate in front and back, plus a rope tied to each end of the front axel for steering and two tin cans for headlights—that was our popular soapbox cart!

One spring we decided to upgrade the rope-steering system by using a castoff steering wheel and a steel rod, but a weld was needed where the steering column met the wheel, and our woodburning tool for woodcrafts proved—as we quickly found—inadequate. But to our good fortune just three blocks down the hill from my house and on Pioneer Street near the east entrance to town stood a large white building with blue trim: Montesano Mercury and Ford.

"I bet we can get a weld there," said one of us.

Having never visited a mechanic's garage, I was surprised how cavern-like and cold it was inside, and how noisy!—with revving motors and clanging metal. The air wasn't good either; nor the sign that said NO UNAUTHORIZED PERSONS ALLOWED.

Of the several cars under repair, one was way up in the air, held by a shiny metal pole thick as a tree, while beside another was an engine in many parts and pieces on the concrete floor. Pulling our cart along, we weaved through the "traffic" and headed for a shower of sparks at the back of the shop.

But on our way to the welder, a mechanic abruptly slid out on a dolly from under a pickup and, looking up at us from the floor, asked what we wanted there.

"We need a weld for the steering wheel of our soapbox cart. This is our 1952 model," we replied.

The mechanic stood up, pulled out a blue grease-splotched rag from his back pocket, wiped his hands on it, put the rag back in his pocket, and slowly walked around our cart. He took a long time inspecting it, tugging on the wheels, studying the peach crate-plank assembly, and the steering mechanics.

"You kids built this?" he inquired.

"Yes, Sir," we said proudly.

He looked it over some more, and then glanced toward two men in suits who were talking by a door marked OFFICE; then he looked at his watch.

"And my dad has a Ford," I added hopefully.

"Well, in that case . . ."

9 SWIMMING THE WYNOOCHE

IN THE HOT summer months, we swam regularly at Lake Sylvia State Park, a magical lake a mile from town created when a dam was built for a sawmill on Sylvia Creek more than a century ago. We also swam in the Pacific Ocean at Grayland and Copalis, where the beaches were smooth and sandy for miles, and the dunes behind perfect for Cowboys & Indians; and in most of the major rivers (all but one with an Indian name) of the Olympic Peninsula on family fishing and camping trips. My sister and I especially loved swimming at Olympic Hot Springs far in the mountains along wild Boulder Creek at the big log lodge with the wood cabins, wood stoves, and the waterwheel that generated electricity for the resort. Swimming there in the hot-spring pools on cold, clear summer nights—wood smoke and steam rising to spectacular mountain stars—for that all I could say was thank you, Life!

We, my gang of friends and I, were, indeed, a rare species of fish in the summer months. We wore our swimsuits under our patched-on-the-knees jeans through the season, ready at the sight of water to jump right in whether a reed-ringed duck pond or some kid's inflated plastic pool (if not too yellow with urine). We loved running through the rainbows of lawn sprinklers after we'd been at the lake, or when no moms were free to take us there.

One nearby and memorable place we swam was the cold Wynoochee River west of town. There we swam offshore with inner tubes beneath a creosoted railroad trestle south of the main highway that ran from Montesano to Aberdeen, where the river was deep and jade-colored, not far from where it flowed into the meandering, log-boomed Chehalis River, a river too industrial for swimming.

The river went under a green, Elector Set-like bridge on Highway 101, then flowed through acre after acre of farmland, mustard and clover and cows, and made a bend around a rise in the land and passed under the railroad trestle where we swam. We never swam there alone; usually several moms would take us. The water was the coldest of any water I swam (except maybe the Hoh or Queets Rivers on camping trips), but it was so clear it could hypnotize you. Our moms dressed in swimsuits too, but they usually stayed on the shore sunning, talking, listening to portable radios, and watching out (they said) that we didn't drown. We used inner tubes to kick out into mid-stream, and then would let the river carry us down to a place where we could catch an eddy and could easily paddle to shore.

Some of the high school kids jumped off the railroad trestle into the deepest water of the river, but we could never get permission from our moms to do that (and I didn't like the look of it anyway).

The water was so cold it was hard to get in without wading around and summoning plenty of courage. After the feet and legs went numb, and the water came up to my belly button, an inner debate was usually precipitated. "Now dive in!"

"I don't know how to dive."

"Then fall in."

"It's too cold. I might black out from shock."

"Get in the water, chicken."

"I'm not a chicken."

"Cluck, cluck, cluck."

And so on.

I did learn, however, later that the best way in is to put your ankles and wrists in the water first—they're like thermostats, Mrs. Baylor told us—and then just plunge in. I had a habit of getting ready to jump in and then backing off, as I said, edging up to the big moment and again backing off. I could wear myself out sometimes trying to get in the river or lake. I would clench my fists and look at the sky and ask, "Is this fair?"

I always thought there must be a painless way to get in, but I never found it, though I understood the word "chicken."

Fortunately, it was when there were no girls around that I had the worst bouts of cold feet, no pun intended. If there were girls around or an obnoxious boy rival, a friend, I found immediate inspiration to throw myself into the freezing waters. Once in, it was necessary to kick and swim as hard as possible to out-swim the Arctic shock. In time, I could flip over on my back like an otter, spout water from my mouth like a seal, and call to anyone still on shore, "Hey, you faint hearts, come on in, the water's fine!" If I had ever gone down to the banks of the Wynooche unescorted and with no one there, I'd probably still be standing up to my knees in the river, shivering like an Indian boy on a vision quest, waiting for a spirit that was powerless to show itself to just a wader.

Be that as it may, swimming in the pure cold waters of the Wynooche was, in fact, related to something like joy, *and* something like a vision. With a few white puffs of clouds in the sky and the summer sun beating down, being in the arms of that beautiful flowing current, feeling the icy water sweeping one's inner tube quietly but firmly away toward the mighty Chehalis and ultimately—if you fell asleep on your inner tube—the sea; making that circuit from under the railroad trestle down to where the river spun out an eddy, tramping back along the breezy shore, and then again launching the inner tube under the railroad trestle, well . . . we did it over and over and over again.

10 A THREE-LETTER WORD FOR THE LARGE OVA OF BIRDS

I HAD PASSED through two and a half grades before I finally misspelled a word on a spelling test. It was around February with snow on the ground and I had been sailing through Mrs. Kemp's spelling tests with the confidence of a Caesar who had more soldiers at his beck than there are people in our town.

By the time we got into spelling bees in the fourth grade, I was permanently eliminated as the top, and maybe even as *one* of the top, spellers. David Gowen, whose father owned the Little Store (our candy store) near the high school ascended to the first chair of spelling and never relinquished that coveted position. He was so unassuming about it, I figured he was a blood heir somehow to the throne.

By the fifth grade my spelling had deteriorated to the point where I was just thankful to stick around through several rounds. David was always the last kid standing there against the windows that faced out on Spruce Street; everyone else defeated, sent in ignominy back to their wooden desk stockades.

"David, spell *xerophilus*."

"Sure."

"Mike, spell *disestablishmentarian*."

"Huh?"

"David?"

"Sure."

Being sent back to our seats in defeat reminded me of the game Bombardment, wherein two teams face off against one another from opposite sides of the gym. The game begins with all the balls being placed on the mid-court line. The players, who start from the farthest ends of their respective sides of the court, rush forward at the P.E. teacher's whistle and race to the balls. The object of the game is to throw a ball and hit someone on the opposing side. A player cannot cross the middle line, and whoever does not catch a ball thrown at him, but is hit by it, is out of the game.

Now very early on, I learned that to rush out first and attempt to grab a ball very likely led to getting hit at close quarters. All the kids running out to grab a ball and get a quick shot at someone were obviously just asking to be clobbered. That wouldn't be so bad, except then you were out of the game, reduced to standing on the sidelines for what could take the whole recess to complete (like being sent back to your seat to watch a spelling bee go on without you.)

If this had been the days of Napoleon or General Lee, your being first in line to be hammered would have possibly got you a medal, or it certainly would have got you dead, which got you—if you believed the propaganda—heaven. But getting plowed down in that first skirmish to reach the balls only got you placed on the sidelines with nothing to do but twiddle your thumbs and watch everyone smarter or luckier than you have fun.

No. My strategy was learned early and it wasn't complicated. Let other kids—brave though some might be—rush up to mid-court and get hit, and then after that, with both teams depleted in numbers, begin to carefully engage the enemy. I don't think I was the only one who was aware of this strategy. Occasionally a kid might remark snottily, "Why don't you come out from the back line and fight from the beginning?" I never condescended to answer. It was obvious. "Because, I want to keep playing, not stand on the sidelines like an idiot."

No matter how often we played Bombardment, a group from both teams never caught on how to survive. In fact, over time, I began to suspect that a number of the earliest to be hit really didn't like the game in the first place. They might like grabbing a ball and flinging it once, but being pummeled by a volley of balls must have held some unhealthy attraction for them. Others though, making unhappy protest from the sidelines, were just kids who were maybe learning something about the laws of evolution.

Fortunately, David Gowen was a self-effacing kid; and I was never so much jealous of him as I was jealous of not being able to stand where he stood, alone, there against the light of the windows, the whole class awe-struck and subdued (spellbound) by the sting of the spelling-bee victor.

The word I missed that winter in the third grade in Mrs. Kemp's class, the word that was the beginning of my descent from the heights was *egg*. It's a very simple word, right? But the picturing part of my brain that had served me so well over many months through the introduction of many new words wouldn't turn on. Boy, did I start sweating, there in that wooden desk with the cut-out inkwell and somebody's big head in front of me.

Egg. Say it fast and try to spell it yourself. It's a very strange sound to stand for such an oval shape. In fact when I tried to picture *egg,* not the word, but the chicken's actual shelled creation, the word *oval* flashed on my mind's picture screen, then *Ovaltine,* then *Captain Midnight* which the Ovaltine people sponsored on Saturday mornings when the kids of America took over TV programming.

Egg. Time was running out. *Egg.* The teacher was collecting the exams. The champion speller was behind in punches in the fifteenth round. Fortunately, we hadn't got to the higher grade testing when the teacher, or the test monitor, tells everyone to put down their pencils at the same time (it reminded me of a sheriff telling you to drop your guns) and then begins to collect the exams. No, in this case the teacher was just casually moving up and down the aisles collecting the papers, chatting easily with all the spellers, stopping here and there to glance at our work.

It was all casual because no one was taking the exam with any of the seriousness that I was, including the teacher. I was defending my crown, my championship; no one but I was doing that. I could have written *ego* and it would have been the correct word for the source of my psychological pain, but I didn't know how to spell that either; I didn't know what an ego was.

I was having a kid's heart attack, a think-you're-so-smart attack! But I still had time, yes, I still had my tooth-marked, number 2 lead pencil in my mitt. But that simple, simple word, for the love of me, I just couldn't see it. (Had I been washing out my spelling powers, my brain, with too much television? Or too much Little Store candy?)

Luckily to my immediate right was Tina Meadows, a bright well-kempt girl of eight, and extremely private—I didn't know where she lived or if she had brothers or sisters or pets. (She smelled okay.) With her glasses on, she could read fast, and I'd listened with admiration to her do it many times in our reading circles. We had three reading circles organized on how competent a reader you were. I was in the first circle, even though when I read fast, there was some trouble understanding me. My sister had advised me never to slip into the lower circles or you'd never get out. The pressure of the first circle grew year by year, but I was fortunate that my teachers were sympathetic to my slight speech impediment.

I leaned over the aisle to get a peek at Tina Meadows' exam. I made it kind of a long feigned yawn with arms stretched wide like a seagull's wings, leaning just far enough to see past Tina Meadow's brown springy curls which held no interest for me at this juncture. Though I had never done this before, it was amazing how I knew exactly how to do it. Like learning to talk, learning to protect one's championships came from the sympathetic nervous system—sympathetic because it was on your side.

But the Champion Speller did not feel good doing it. No, the Champ's heart was booming out like the clock tower on the courthouse, and his sweat glands opened like the hungry, fly-seeking mouths of little perch in Hood Canal. This is cheating, I said to myself. *You are now cheating,* the voice within me repeated.

Of course, I'm older now and have learned that cheating is a very minor offense against the rules created by people who are not kids. And cheating, which I do only when absolutely pressed, like lying, is not half as bad as so many things that the things that we cheat against do to the world. (I heard mistakenly my dad say once that everyone cheats on their Texans.) You could almost say that cheating is what makes certain games one cheats at more interesting.

So I leaned (yawned my way) over for a peek at Tina Meadow's paper, and there it was, the word I needed to save me: *agg.*

11 SAINT JOHN

I'M ABOUT TO tell you one of the dumbest things I ever did (I'm on my way), and I can only tell it now because it happened when I was so small it's not a crime punishable by law, and if it were, the statute of recrimination has expired.

John Mobrey, perhaps my dad's best friend, managed Montesano Lumber and Supply. He was older than my dad and bald. He chewed Copenhagen snuff, so I'm sure he was a logger in his younger days. He offered me some once, but I didn't like it. A kid appreciates the offer, though.

He and his wife, Anita, often went camping with us, and even once, all the way to Banff, Canada, where they have grizzly bears, and hot springs to swim in away from the bears; plus that big hotel my Great Uncle Sam built, or at least helped to build, he a bricklayer by trade and a big Irishman. Uncle Sam was my farm grandmother's bachelor brother. He was a fun man who liked to tease my grandmother, who had to be a little strict because after Grandfather died she had to run the farm alone. Uncle Sam would tease her and on occasion would side with us kids against her in trivial disputes.

"You know your grandmother has a boyfriend in Blaine, don't you?"

"Sam, you old scoundrel, don't be talking foolish in front of the children."

That's exactly what Uncle Sam liked to do, talk foolish. And that's exactly what we liked him to do.

Several times I'd been scolded for going into the chicken house and scaring the chickens. It was really something to see and hear a hundred or so chickens—in a storm of straw dust and feathers—squawking and flying crazily all at once. Grandmother scolded me once in front of Uncle Sam. "When you go into the chicken house, you have to be quiet. If the chickens get excited and fly around it lowers their egg production."

Even to me that made sense. But on hearing Grandmother, Uncle Sam said, "Why, Mike, I wouldn't listen to a word your grandmother says. Those old Rhode Island Reds need a little stimulation once in a while. They only have two roosters in there for a hundred hens."

Though I see him rarely, Uncle Sam just proves that being on the side of kids, despite the cards adults stack against it, *it*—siding with kids—can win you in the future—perhaps far in the future, perhaps only after you have gone to heaven—a remembrance and affection from those very kids you humored, at least from some of them who survived long enough to realize that their very sanity and good hearts derive from people like old Uncle Sam. And John Mobrey.

John often came with my dad and me to sports events, even to the district basketball championships in Centralia, where I saw my first glass backboards . . . well, partially saw. John was always fun to have along; he had a great sense of humor that matched my father's. I think they liked each other because at some point in their lives they had decided to laugh at things others had decided to complain about. John also had jokes to tell me, too, which naturally made me feel I was being initiated, not into adulthood, but something more interesting, like friendship.

One fine day my mother took me to John's store, located not far from the Dairy Queen, to buy a bathroom fixture. My sister was along with us, and she and I began to wander among the display appliances, waiting for Mom. There were all kinds of refrigerators, bathtubs, and even some brand new toilets in colors I'd never seen toilets in before. My sister had decided she wanted to open every refrigerator door and peek in and giggle. I found that boring and thought I'd maybe pee in one of the colored display toilets while I was waiting. So I did. My sister finished her Betty Crocker tour of the refrigerators, came over to me, and looked down into the toilet, which I was having difficulty flushing.

Energized, my sister screamed and ran across the room to where Mom was talking to John. Shortly, my mother, piloted by my sister, found her way over to me (my sister dancing up and down in feigned shock and excited expectation) and my mother, red with embarrassment, then white with indignation, asked: "What in heaven's [that would be "hell" in the French masculine] name are you doing?"

I was throttling that toilet handle, that's what I was doing.

"What have you done?"

I thought the yellow vitamin-enriched puddle at the bottom of the bowl spoke for itself. A bad mother might have smacked me a good one, but, heaven be thanked, beatings were not sanctioned in our household (we had no woodshed like the mill or logger families). A really bad mother, though, in the sense of neglectful, could be good if she didn't care enough to do anything one way or the other.

"Little Man, you're going right over to John Mobrey and apologize to him this minute," my mom said. I could tell she was at least getting a measure of control over herself. But that "Little Man" stuff was as good as reading me my rights before taking them away.

I could feel the tears coming, and when tears came in such situations, it always amazed me how you lost all power over your prouder self, but for a moment, through the anguish, came sudden relief because I finally knew who I was without the least ambiguity or confusion, whole and undivided in the great mysterious universe: I was a victim!

I didn't want to move. I didn't want to lose John's respect by either telling him what I'd done, or by his seeing his sports buddy bawling his head off. I kept thinking: Why didn't someone tell me these toilets weren't connected to plumbing? How was a kid to know that? True, I shouldn't have peed in the showcase window, but hey, I'm just a kid, and still largely *tabula rasa*. I'm going to refuse to move from this spot for as long as it takes. ("Sure, Mike, that will really scare them," said the Devil. "You're onto something now, Kid.")

"Here comes John," my mother said. "You apologize this instant."

John appeared from the maze of stoves and refrigerators. "What's up, Shirley?"

"Mike here has something he wants to tell you," my mother said, making it sound like I was a murder suspect about to open a suitcase that contained the heads of all the neighborhood's missing Barbie dolls.

(My sister was dancing between appliances in perfect bliss.) "Oh, you do," said John, glancing first at my pitiful face and then into the white porcelain bowl with the yellow puddle.

"Well, what is it, Mike?" John asked.

I had vowed not to move, which I was adhering to, but I felt compelled to speak. Owing though to my minor speech impediment, particularly noticeable when under emotional stress, I had to say it twice to get it out: "I peed in your display toilet."

"Oh, that," said John. "It's nothing. I do that all the time myself."

12 KID NAPPING

A S A KID you never rest voluntarily. You never go to bed because you want to. Most enforced rests are for the benefit of parents and teachers, or babysitters. Night-to-dawn sleeping took care of all the resting I ever cared to do.

In the earliest grades when you had a little rug with your name on it in the cloakroom for the afternoon nap period, I always wondered where the teacher went. None of us knew for sure. Davy Lewis said they went to the lavatory in the basement. I'd never been in our school's basement, and now I had a reason not to go. Jimmy said that was nonsense, they went to a teacher's lounge somewhere and smoked cigarettes. Sandra Keating once said they just went outside for a breath of fresh air, but we laughed at that because it was always raining. Sandra Keating then changed her mind and said something even stupider, "They go to powder their nose."

We were supposed to be napping like good boys and girls while these conjectures bubbled up from our rug-cushioned brains on the floor. I did use my rug time to some advantage, though, plotting after-school activities: whose ball field to ride over to, what floor of the Fort to work on, or what kid to beat up, etc.

Musing on after-school play, I really wished I could skip changing shirts, pants, and shoes, which cost me both the time to get home before going out again and the time it took to change. Patched-in-the-knees jeans, tennis shoes, an old corduroy shirt or sweatshirt, a lucky rabbit foot, and a ball cap—that's all I needed to feel like a great kid, it was all I needed to be a great kid!

Going home directly from school, though, was perilous because you might get broadsided with "time to get a haircut," or "time to clean your room."

One kid wet his pants while taking the enforced nap causing a major hubbub. Another time little Alice Winkler threw up. I was goofing around myself once during naptime and knocked over the girls' beloved playhouse. Fortunately, no one was in it, it being naptime, or I might have killed my first people.

Usually, though, nothing happened except a lot of squirming and gentle snoring. When the full lights came on again and the teacher returned, most of us stood up slowly and yawned like lion cubs, pretending we had just been awakened from a hundred years of sleep, suggesting we wished we could nap on our rugs forever.

This performance always seemed to please the teacher. Her good children had been completely conk-O and didn't hear her sneaking in or out; didn't hear her up in the principal's office requesting from Duke Elmsworth a transfer to another school, or putting powder on her nose, as Sandra Keating not, perhaps, so stupidly suggested.

Some kids enjoyed the naps, especially farm kids who lived way up the Wynooche River and had to travel on the school bus for an hour each day, and who had to do chores in the morning about the same time as the robins warbled their first notes of the traditional rain song, Montesano's anthem. Eddy Barkley, from upper Wynooche was a snorer, so I know he must have been enjoying rug time. Some of the girls at nap time went out like a string of lights on a Christmas tree, a defective string made in Japan, and I know this because sometimes I'd whisper to Belinda Waters, a cute girl who skipped rope like a maniac, but Belinda, on her rug in front of me was always out like a sack of Sunkist oranges the moment her blonde pigtails hit the floor.

With the teacher back in the classroom and the lights on, we all folded up our rugs and climbed into our desk seats. Facing new math problems or a really boring story of some obscure figure of Washington State history who got rich trading, not trapping, furs, we had to wonder sometimes if we had wasted an opportunity by staying awake during nap time.

But, hey, by contrast to nap time, did I love recess? That was about the best time in my day, though it only lasted fifteen minutes. Our hearts thumped with joy as we rushed out into the big concrete playground for kickball or softball or, if the weather was bad, into the shining halls of the Little Gym for wrestling, dodgeball, or relay races.

What pained us, though, were the times our recess got preempted by practice for the May Festival. Each grade spent all their precious recess time practicing, practicing the group routines to perform for parents at the big May event. Of course, we got no vote in this, and the girls certainly liked it all much better than we boys. One year, the boys' part was to wear monkey outfits and scamper around the gym floor while an audience of millions looked on in amusement. Oh, we monkeys, with our long wired-up tails, were a big hit all right. The parents just about fell out of the bleachers guffawing. There were so many flashbulbs popping that we monkeys darn near went blind. One of us managed to get his tail snagged in the fluffy costume of one of the girls on the floor doing the routine (if you can call it that) with us (I can't remember what made monkeys and girls in fluffy costumes go together). Our tails consisted of material woven round a stiff pliable wire. The boy's tail hooked the girl's costume (now I recall, the girls were supposed to be tropical birds; it was a tropical theme) and then scampered away with a part of the girl's costume, her wings. This changed everything. The little wingless girl ran bawling to the gym exit, the faces of the adults went from comic to tragic. (May Day, indeed!)

With the music still playing, we monkey kids just continued scampering—what else could we do? But it was getting awfully warm inside our goofy costumes.

Finally, the music stopped and, instead of the usual tumultuous, child-adoring applause that met the end of each performance, we received a tepid ovation. Which was okay by me because I sure didn't want an encore.

13 QUEEN FOR A DAY

I T WAS QUITE a few years before I liked to eat my lunch at school. Some older kid said I was tied to my mother's apron strings. He didn't live two blocks from school like I did, or maybe he would have been tied to them too (*his* mother's, that is).

The fact is I hated buying my lunch at school. I was always losing the dog-eared punch cards, and then there was that long snaking line of hungry students formed up the stairs from the basement cafeteria. There was also that weird cooking smell unlike any smell ever found in our kitchen at home, or at the Bee Hive Koffee Shop. Consistently the cafeteria served up meatloaf rather than honest hamburger; the vegetables included pulpy kidney beans and tasteless peas; and the pudding served for dessert always had about an inch of skin covering it like on a stagnant pond.

When I did eat my lunch at school, I preferred to stay in the classroom and eat the lunch my mother had made and packed neatly in my lunch box. I can still smell the interior of that tin lunch pail: a lonely smell because I wouldn't be eating at home with Mom, but also a consoling smell because I wouldn't be eating in the school cafeteria.

My lunch box had a clip that held the thermos of milk and ample room for two sandwiches wrapped in wax paper, and in the corners, cookies, carrot sticks, fresh celery, and a napkin. Sometimes Mom would top things off with an apple, an orange, or a hard-boiled egg. It wasn't what was known as a "hot lunch," but it had a very good record of staying down once you ate it.

Truth was I much preferred walking home the two blocks, via alleys, to have lunch with Mom. Toasted tuna sandwiches with melted cheese were often the reward of that two-block journey. I also liked bologna or egg salad sandwiches with a bowl of noodle or tomato soup, and crackers. With my lunch before me, my mother and I would click on the table radio and listen to *Queen for a Day*.

Some show that. All these women with problems telling in public their horrid stories so they could become Queen for a Day. I'd never heard of such suffering. The thing I didn't like about it was in order to win, a woman had to suffer more than anyone else. It was just the opposite of a contest of merit; it was based on misery. On occasion though, a contestant wouldn't have a big problem at all. For example, one woman wanted money to buy a fence to keep her neighbor's dog from pooping in her yard. On a scale of suffering, I figured she rated a 1. But on the other hand, one woman wanted money to give to a doctor to save her little girl who was growing hair all over her face. According to the woman, it was a rare disease that nobody but her daughter had. She lost to a woman who had had her foot crushed in an elevator door and needed money to fix it (her foot, not the door).

That day I was rooting for the hairy-faced girl because I knew she would find it hard to make friends at school if she looked like a hay field. My mother reassured me, though, that just because someone doesn't win Queen for a Day doesn't mean they won't find help elsewhere. This was reassuring because I was just a little afraid that someday I might run into that little girl on the street.

Blind women, by the way, were most popular contestants with the audiences, and it was the audience that voted the winners by their applause. One blind woman, who wanted a seeing-eye dog, said if she had one she'd be able to go to Safeway and eat better. She received thunderous applause and deserved to be Queen for a Day, or,

I'd say, for even a week. In addition to the seeing-eye dog—which, I presumed, they had to order from a pound—she received a scenic cruise to the Mediterranean that, perhaps, would have been a better prize for the woman with the hairy-faced daughter. They also gave the blind queen a mink coat and a silver necklace, which she could wear when her new dog took her grocery shopping.

After Queen for a Day, it was high noon and I'd hurry back to school under big white clouds piled up over the green trees of the hills south of town. I'd be heading straight for the playfield for marbles or kickball. It was out in the playfield where David Contee had a seizure and got to rolling around in the ditch by the iron mesh fence. It was one of the scariest things I'd ever seen, and at the time, none of us knew what was happening. David didn't look like he knew either. And the playfield got so quiet, it was like someone had pulled the plug on the world.

Luckily, one of the teachers knew what was happening and helped David when he came to his senses. Like polio, drowning, and car accidents (not to mention the A-bomb we'd seen go off in the Civil Defense movie), fits were just one more thing to add to our list of things we were learning we had better not think too much about because they all added up to trouble and suffering, and as kids, we imagined we'd had enough of that in our lives maybe already. And we sure didn't want to become some kind of candidate on Queen, King, or Prince for a Day.

14 THE GUNS OF MONTESANO

A S A KID, guns were an essential element of life in Montesano. I toted two pistols, six shooters, in twin studded holsters, and sometimes when the fighting was heavy, packed a Winchester rifle.

As I grew up I made it a point to bring law and order to my neighborhood and especially to "playing guns" itself. The tendency of kids new to guns was to shoot and shoot willy-nilly. Since there were five churches within a block of my home, we often used their porches and surrounding trees and shrubbery for gunfights (the irony was lost on us; maybe we should have played Crusades). When I say I brought law and order to gunplay in my neighborhood, I mean I rescued "playing guns" from devolving into random shoot-outs so anarchical you couldn't determine if you killed anyone or if you were killed. Just going BANG-BANG or BLAM-BLAM all over the place was ludicrous, was pre-school.

I felt early on that there had to be consequences for being shot, ambushed, or out manned. The rules I implemented included that if you were shot before you could shoot the other kid, then you were officially dead and had to stay dead for at least the count of thirty. If the kid was small and couldn't count to thirty, well, stay dead as long as it takes you to sing three stanzas of "Davy Crockett, King of the Wild Frontier," or long enough to let the gunslinger who shot you ride off on his horse around the corner of the church.

That was the rule I implemented (to general approval) in the event only a few kids were playing guns. But if quite a few kids were playing, we divided into good guys and bad guys, Indians and cowboys, or those who liked Roy Rogers and those who liked Gene Autry, or those whose parents had Fords and those who had Chevrolets, or those who liked the Dodgers and those who liked the Yankees, or those who liked Stevenson and those who liked Ike, or those who liked the Washington State Cougars or those who liked the Washington Huskies, and then when you got shot, you had to be dead until another member of your gang, or race, or neighborhood touched you. This rule cleared up one thing perfectly: the shoot-out was over when all of one side or the other was dead.

There were other important rules enforced as well. No machineguns, for instance. No firecrackers, no crying. No girls (this was symbolic only, because I don't remember any girls ever wanting to play—and certainly not guns—with us). No throwing your gun at somebody. No tying up gunslingers you've shot or hanging them. No shooting at passers-by. No shooting someone while they peed. And no wandering out past prescribed boundaries, for example, no leaving one church for another.

Unlike real life, "playing guns" allowed that after you'd killed a whole gang of shooters, the gang's members came back to life. And it wasn't so bad getting shot yourself under the properly staged circumstances. No one liked to be surprised from the bushes—POW-POW you're dead! You lost face for being surprised and suddenly, because of the rules, dead. Waiting for someone on your side to come and touch you and bring you back to life was also excruciating. And you weren't supposed to move, or pee, or shout for help either.

But say you were high up on a church porch, surrounded by several kids of a bad posse (the Gene Autrys, Chevys, or Yankees, for instance) moving stealthily in on you below. Knowing they had the numbers, and had scouted you out, you staged a death. Like maybe rushing down the steps shooting wildly until they mowed you down on the green lawn. You might even take a long time to fall on the ground and die, which was within the rules, just so long as you ultimately kicked the bucket. Or, being shot off that same porch, but falling over the railing and landing dead in a big bush—preferably not one too prickly—that landscaped a particular church. Of course, we had the Great Neighborhood Bean-Shooting War, and went for a while with water balloons and even rocks (though we implemented a ban on rocks as well). Slingshots were quickly outlawed after one kid took a rock on his chin, and BB guns were never used except on dogs and birds, and then only by poor kids with unhappy parents.

We played guns in the woods; we played guns in the streets when they tore them up and left mounds of dirt and big ditches and tunnels; we played guns on the church grounds as I said, but we never played guns at school. And we played guns at construction sites amid the newly framed structures and the fresh-smelling lumber piles.

When a bit older and I'd pass a perfect site for guns, I'd grow wistful and reach for my holsters (figuratively speaking), which I didn't even know where they went or when. Those toy guns just disappeared into thin air when I wasn't somehow thinking about them much anymore. Maybe my parents took them away in the night as they had done with my favorite blanket when I was very tiny, about the size of a bullfrog. Or, perhaps I pawned them for a leather-bound volume of Shakespeare's Sonnets.

In truth, what happens to a young cowboy's guns is he usually trades them in for a gun that really works. When you think about it, that's how a hunter comes to be, probably. It certainly seems to be how a soldier arises. If you don't make it hunting or soldiering than you can have guns if you're a crook. Lots of crooks have guns, though not all guns are in the hands of crooks.

Given enough time a kid grows up and the cowboy who you once thought you were and enjoyed being in the past rides off into the sunset. Then—without a shot—the cowboy within you is dead, mostly.

15 THE PIANIST

I HAD HEARD my sister practicing in the piano room for more than a year; I'd also watched Jimmy Dockers practice at his house and heard that Randy Hopkins was learning too. Miss Stickles was their teacher, and she was touted by everyone in Montesano as the best. But the piano bug took longer to bite me. I'd tried acrobatics, tap dancing, tumbling, and didn't like them. No, I would just stick to the seasonal, the major, sports, thank you, and fishing, swimming, and bike riding. But listening to my sister play so well, the music wore my resistance down. I started lessons and surprisingly took to the music the way a duck takes to water. Among other things, I found reading notes very fascinating, as I would later find the Periodic Table of Elements. Translating sheet music into songs was alchemy. I came to appreciate the ancient composers too: Bach, Mozart, Chopin. I wasn't doing bad.

About this time, Liberace was becoming a big hit on television, along with his brother, George. I watched their show all the way through only once, though my mother and her friends were nuts about it. Liberace played the piano when he wasn't talking with George, and he did both with a big honeyed grin. There were always candelabra with burning candles on his grand piano and exotic flowers set around the stage for atmosphere. I think this is what Montesano called high culture.

My practice continued for several months. Outside at the piano room window, Terry or Johnny Rachet would sometimes tap and hold up a football. It hurt my sense of team duty, team *esprit* to shake my head and mouth the words: "I can't come out; I have to practice." I didn't mind practicing really; I just hated to deny the Rachet brothers their recruitment. In sparsely populated Montesano, we kids always dreamed of having enough players to fill out teams to the standard or official complement. To have eleven against eleven for sandlot football would have been, for instance, several city blocks beyond wonderful. There was some kind of code among sports kids I was breaking by being unavailable. But as a young artist, I had sheet music to interpret, chords to play, and tunes to perfect.

Then came my first recital at the parlor of Miss Stickle's old home. Several of us beginners were on the program, and our moms politely came to watch. I played several short *con brio* classical pieces, and then, to applause, made the courteous bow that Miss Stickles had taught, and required of, us. Everything was fine. I even gave a second, and a third bow. I was beginning to catch the drift of the muscial culture.

Then Miss Stickles—very pleased with it all—thanked me and spoke a few words to the mothers. "Mike has learned to play so very well in such a short time. I have a strong feeling that if he continues to work hard, he will someday be a fine pianist."

PEE-A-NIST! That word flew right out of Miss Stickles' mouth, shot to the left in mid-air and struck me like an arrow between the eyes. It was as if someone had shouted fire in the middle of a piano recital.

PEE-A-NIST! I couldn't believe my ears. Then the mothers gave me another round of applause! I was on my way (if I continued to work hard) to becoming a PEE-A-NIST, which was exactly what my mom and her friends called LIBERACE. And he sure seemed to me to be one—a PEE-A-NIST—through and through. I don't know what they called his brother George, but I can tell you I wasn't going to be one of them either.

I refused to practice from that day forth. At the very height of my success as a child prodigy (that might be overstating things), I was closing the lid on the piano keyboard and locking up my metronome. My mother and father, and even my sister, entreated me to continue playing, but I was as set in my mind as a hook should be set in a rainbow trout.

After sitting in the piano room for a couple of weeks without playing so much as a few notes of "Chopsticks," I was released by my parents to the green grass and trees of the backyard. There I found my old neighborhood friends again, and soon forgot the whole musical interlude.

Or so I thought. Much later, I realized I was pretty dumb about the whole thing. Don't ever let anyone tell you that words, even a single word, don't have powerful influences. Although I learned other instruments along the way, the truth is, I missed piano. It seemed to really suit me. Maybe late in life I'll get back to it, but it's too late now to be as good as I really could have been. If there had just been some way I had been referred to as just a piano player or if Liberace and his brother had just stayed on the radio, maybe things would have worked out.

I don't blame my parents, specifically my mother, for any of this. What could she do? Torture or starve me until I started up with the scales again. That is one secret of kids, for better or worse: if they ever make up their mind to something and really absolutely are determined to stick it out, there isn't much anyone can do about it. (Of course, one must assume that we are talking about decent families that do not resort to torture, beatings, and starvation. "Oh, Johnny, so you don't want to practice, do you? Let me just see if I can pull some of the hair out of your eyebrows.")

16 HERSCHEL, CHESS MASTER

M Y MOTHER WAS good friends with Catherine Philips, who begat two sons, Paul, the younger, a little older than I, who became my friend, and Arthur, much older than I, who was a genius and, by some standards, an eccentric.

Catherine was married to Herschel, who was a logger, but Herschel didn't seem to work as much as other loggers, or other fathers. During summer vacation, Herschel could always be found at home smoking a pipe, wearing old slippers, and reading novels. More than once I overheard parents mentioning him as "a good enough fellow, but, my god, does he ever work? And Catherine . . . she just knocks herself out at the hospital. What a trooper, that gal. And I never hear her complain about Herschel. And what about that house of theirs? It just sits there across Paradise Creek without a coat of paint. You'd think in his spare time, which is ample, he might at least paint the porch, or the steps. And let's not forget, Arthur, that older son. Now there's an odd one."

"Arthur is different, perhaps, but I must say he is something of a wizard with mechanical and electrical things. Catherine sent him over to fix our TV, and he took it apart in ten minutes and put it back together in five. We've had good reception ever since, and we even pick up Canadian stations. Arthur may be different, but I prefer him coming to the house over Ben 'Lover Boy' Turner from the TV and radio shop."

"Well, you've got a point there. The last time Ben Turner came to our house, I felt I might have to call the police the way he hung around all day and drank his thermos coffee. Worse, he never fixed the TV right and he charges an arm and a leg."

It was during the summer between fourth and fifth grade that I ran with Paul. I should say "rode" because we both were into long bicycle adventures, especially on the old highway: from Montesano to Brady, and from Montesano to Aberdeen (and back, of course). We both had speedometers mounted on our bikes (on my Columbia and on Paul's Schwinn) and our goal was to ride so far during summer that our speedometers would reach a thousand miles. We had no idea what would happen when the mileage became higher than our speedometers could record. Hence, we rode with a kind of religious fervor toward the unfathomable apocalyptic thousand-mile moment. But like our efforts to produce a good stock of flavored toothpicks, we fell short of our vision—a thousand miles was too far to go under the illusion that going that far, piling up the mileage, mattered. But we did ride all over the place that summer, and to get started early on a number of journeys, I often stayed at Paul's.

One morning, Paul and I passed through his living room on our way to the kitchen. Mr. Philips was already in his favorite reading chair and wearing the robe and slippers he'd worn the evening before. When we returned with our bowls of milk and cereal (Paul preferred Kellogg's Corn Flakes while I was devoted to Cheerios) to the dining room, Mr. Philips came over to us and placed a checkerboard and chess pieces on the table before us. "How would you boys like to learn chess?"

That was the start of days of lessons and matches. During our apprenticeship, Mr. Philips got called back to work. He was gone seven or eight days, and when he came home he looked completely different in his sweat-stained hickory shirt, tin hat, and muddy cork boots. We had thought we were maybe losing our chess master for the rest of the summer, but Grays Harbor weather had turned dangerously hot even for August, and someone in authority had shut down the woods owing to the fire hazard.

Mr. Philips quickly resumed his place as eminent chess master, wearing the pipe, slippers, and robe we knew him best in. I still play the royal game, but I'm a much weaker player than I was in the days studying with Herschel. He taught us well enough that we could really make him pause and think sometimes how to move. His son, Paul, even beat him a few times which delighted Herschel. It was kind of him to share so many secrets with us that we so eagerly used against him and others later. He really wanted us to beat him, is what we felt, but that wasn't the same thing as his *letting* us beat him.

"Oh, Herschel's nice enough, but, god, that Studebaker Catherine has to drive to work; I swear, when it passes the house, it sounds like a big bucket of rivets."

"Ha, ha. I thought you said rickets, 'a bucket of *rickets.*'"

"No. *Rivets.* And the poor gal has to drive it ten miles every day to the hospital in Aberdeen, and sometimes in the middle of the night."

After the summer of chess and the thousand-miles-or-bust campaign, a different kind of gossip circulated. Someone had been stealing women's underwear from the backyard clotheslines in Montesano. When I overheard this, I remembered Davy Lewis, my mischievous classmate, who once stole a white shirt from his neighbor's clothesline, ripped it up, and used the rags for the tail of his kite. But beyond that, the specific theft of women's underwear was new.

"Well, you know what I think," said a friend of my mom's to my mom. "I think it could be that elder son of the Philips', you know who I mean . . ."

"Arthur!?"

"Yes, Arthur. It wouldn't surprise me the least if he's the one."

"Oh, I don't think so, Emma. He's a little unusual , but very well mannered. He's often fixed our washing machine or our TV. My husband insisted on paying him, but he said he wouldn't take money for something so easy. No, if you're looking for the weirdo snatching underwear, I'd suggest considering Ben Turner at the TV shop, or . . . whatshisname from the library."

Because Arthur was shy and reclusive, not many got to know him the way I did as a guest of his brother. For one thing, no one in town knew that he was certified as a Ham Radio operator. His big radio set was in the corner of his room otherwise occupied by a ton of science books and the most complex electric train set I'd ever seen.

Arthur, seated at his radio equipment with a small lamp on, could talk to people all over the world, even in Oregon. Then in the middle of the night, he might start all his trains up at once, and have them running pell-mell through a most intricate molded landscape of plaster of paris mountains, lakes, and townships. The several tracks wove around each other, plunged into tunnels and crossed bridges, the trains tooting and whistling, pulling into little stations to load water, coal, uranium, firewood, passengers, etc.

I'd had a simple American Flyer train set, and all it did—or all I could constructively think of making it do—was go around and around in an oval at varying speeds. To spice things up, I got into the train-wrecking mode, putting toy soldiers on the tracks and running them over with the train at full throttle. I carried out quite a few executions and derailments before my American Flyer (I still remember it was painted a very nice indigo) flew forever apart. This destructiveness, while somehow satisfying a lower instinct in me, might also have signaled an anti-technology strain. No, it was just fun sometimes to wreck things rather than make them. I was too young, though, to get much beyond the realization that wrecking things, however satisfying to that lower instinct, usually made others, usually parents, very unhappy. Consequently, giving satisfaction to the lower instinct in charge of wrecking things—once you'd been punished sufficiently—was carried out on a smaller, covert scale—and usually where and when you wouldn't get caught.

By contrast to my train set, Arthur's was spectacular. The time and care Arthur had taken to create it, with so much detail and ingenuity, must have been equal to a school year. If the gossipmongers of the town had known about Arthur's trains, they'd have known he didn't have any interest or time to be stealing underwear. He was too busy being stationmaster!

Sometimes, when Arthur had all the different trains running like crazy, he'd get a call on his Ham Radio from someone and right away, like a great maestro, he'd slow all the trains down to a sweet railroad hum and focus on his communications. I don't know when Arthur ever slept. Paul and I would finally fall asleep across the hall, lulled by the sound of night trains passing through Arthur World.

For as long as I lived in Montesano, the Philips' house never got painted; Herschel never became a steady member of the workforce; and Arthur graduated from high school and went into the Navy as an electrical engineer. When the Studebaker died, Catherine switched from working at the Catholic hospital in Aberdeen to a local doctor's clinic in town. And Paul went on riding his bike toward the Big Moment without me.

The clothesline thief was never apprehended. But one day, we caught Achilles, the Mayor's German Shepherd, in a neighbor's backyard with a piece of fresh laundry in his teeth. He was snarling and fighting that clothes article like it was a cat. But it was certainly doubtful he, a dog, could distinguish among the items of clothing those specifically that were making all the women in town nervous. Nonetheless, even if Achilles had been the source of the hubbub, in other words, the underwear thief, we kids would never have squealed on a dog.

17 401

WHEN I FIRST heard of 401, I didn't quite understand it; then I didn't quite believe it when I thought I understood it. Billy Pollard, an older kid, was the first I heard explain it just after a noon match of marbles in the playground. It was an older kids' circle or ringer game and I was part of the huddle admiring Billy Pollard's technique.

Billy Pollard was cleaning up. He couldn't miss from inside or outside the big chalk-drawn circle. With a grin on his face as wide as the Cheshire Cat's, he put the marbles he'd won into his jeans pockets, and announced, "I'm going to win the marble tournament in Aberdeen."

Another older kid quipped, "Don't forget to visit 401."

All the older kids laughed. I wanted to ask, "What's 401?" but thought better of it. David Cassidy, a boy in my class, and brave for his age, however, did ask, "What's 401?" And all the older kids laughed again.

"Hey, cut it out," David said, standing his ground. "Tell us what's 401."

"Sure," said Billy Pollard, pockets bulging with marbles. "Why not. Though the information won't be of any use to a fourth grader."

The older boys all laughed again.

"Just tell us," said David.

"Sure. Since everybody in the whole world already knows: 401 is a whorehouse in Aberdeen."

Everyone laughed again.

I didn't know what a whorehouse was, so I went on standing there eager to be schooled. David was unruffled. "I got a good idea what that is, but why don't you edify us."

Edify. That was David—tough and smart.

"Sure," the older boy said, enjoying the spotlight. "401 Water Street in Aberdeen is the address of a whorehouse. A whorehouse is where all the girls run around naked."

The chorus of older boys roared again, and a few of us younger kids, trying to appear older, joined in. But then—having had a second to consider what the older kid had said—I stopped and blurted out, "Run around naked?" Immediately I bit my tongue. Everyone turned and looked at me.

"That's right," an older boy said. "A whole bunch of girls live in the same house together and run around naked. That's a whorehouse."

"Big deal," said David. "My three sisters live in our house and run around at least half naked all the time."

"Well maybe you should give us your address," the older boy said.

David doubled his fists and took a threatening step toward the older boy, but just then the end-of-lunch-hour bell rang.

"Saved by the bell," someone shouted.

That afternoon, a warm stuffy one in the crowded schoolroom, I tried to focus my attention on what our teacher, Mrs. Sable, was trying to teach us, but I kept drifting back through my mind to what had been disclosed on the playground. It was rather strange the way my mind was working. Images of a house with naked girls running all over the place kept popping up. I could almost make out their bottoms, but the picture was incomplete. They—the naked-girl images in my mind—would run up some stairs, then down. Some ran into the kitchen and others the living room to listen naked to the radio. It was definitely new dream territory. I'd compare it to a garden, where for a while there are only seeds hidden in the soil. You knew the garden as you had seen it lying fallow there for some time. Then one day there are new things growing in it and you don't know where they came from and you aren't even sure what they are. The idea of a bunch of girls listening to a radio naked in Aberdeen . . . well, it was a new plant species that had sprung up in my garden overnight, and I wasn't sure if it was a weed, a fruit, or a vegetable.

II.

One spring in the fifth grade, I and a couple other fifth graders had made, barely, the sixth-grade softball team. We didn't get to play much, but we did for the first time get to travel to a few other schools with the older boys to play.

The whole team boarded the bus in the early afternoon and headed for Aberdeen to play Cosmopolis on a neutral field (Cosmopolis was evidently so small they had to borrow a baseball field from Aberdeen). It was pretty exciting to be taking the trip with the older boys and maybe, because I was small, they'd put me in the game at some point to draw a walk. I couldn't hit well yet, but I could crouch down real low and narrow the strike zone enough that my on-base percentage wasn't bad.

"Take off your jacket, O'Connor; we need a man on."

"I get to hit?" I asked from the bench.

"You bet, but don't swing at anything."

"Even if it's a fat pitch?"

"Squat low and take every pitch."

When we reached Central Park, a sort of town midway between Aberdeen and Montesano, which was so small—even smaller than Cosmopolis—we didn't think anyone lived there, some of the players started talking about 401. It had dawned on them, and then on me, that we would be passing by 401 just after we got to the other side of the big counterweighted drawbridge spanning the Wishkah River at the entrance to Aberdeen. Coach Clemens was having a conversation with the driver and the team manager at the front of the bus, and he didn't notice that a number of his baseball squad was stealing across the aisle to sit on the left side of the bus.

You've guessed it: the left side of the bus was the side of the 401 residence. As the bus approached Aberdeen, one of the smarter boys shooed every one back to their seats, as it was beginning to look suspicious, if the coach had looked, to see just me and a couple other fifth graders seated on the right side of the bus.

"I'll give the signal," the older kid said. "Then everyone can take a look." He and a couple other kids also stealthily opened a bunch of the windows.

We went up over the drawbridge into Aberdeen, crossing the steel grating that opened for ships, and as we rolled down the other side, a row of mostly abandoned weathered houses of settlement-Aberdeen times came into view. The smart older boy gave a signal of "okay" and everyone, myself included, flung themselves into the seats on the left side of the bus and struggled in the pile-up to get their heads out the windows as far as they could without falling out of the bus. We were all wearing baseball caps and some of the team lost theirs out the windows.

Sure enough, we could read the number 401 on the porch of the house. "There it is!" someone shouted; but the house was as empty as a movie theater on Sunday morning. It must have been the oddest of sights, if anyone had been there to witness, to see a yellow school bus filled with clamoring baseball kids hanging out the windows, passing by that whorehouse. Empty whorehouse. Former whorehouse? For one brief moment I thought I actually saw someone peeking out from behind a yellow roll-curtain in the upstairs window, but actually the upstairs windows were all boarded up. It must have been my developing imagination.

Then the bus began making a sharp right turn at the corner, and the weight of all of us lumped up on the left side tipped the bus perilously over on only its two left wheels. The bus teetered there, then went all the way over on its side and crashed and slid in a terrible screeching of metal and sparks down the street into a telephone pole and blew up. Everyone was killed instantly, except for the driver, team manager, and coach.

That's how a guilty conscience might write the end. But actually our bus rolled past 401 without incident (other than the coach barking at us to sit down) and we arrived at the ballpark thinking only of line drives and homers (or in my case, walks).

18 RAIN

WHEN IT RAINS in Montesano, it changes everything as night changes day. The world can be going along like a circus, or even just a small carnival, and then, with big dark-bellied clouds rolling in from the coast, the circus stops (or the small carnival) and hurriedly takes down the big top, packs up the trapeze, gets the elephants in line, sobers up the monkeys, puts clothes on the tattooed man, and splits town.

After a couple days of rain rinsing shingles, shredding maple leaves, and forming ponds on most playfields, we kids changed, too. My sister, being bookish (and smart), was positively euphoric about rain. She'd take me under her umbrella (at least a little way) to the nearby library, and we'd come home with armsful of books. I think the rain (and, yes, my sister) is the reason I came to see in books an alternative to living without them.

In addition to reading, though, the rain held us indoors for all kinds of activities too numerous to list here. Well, here's some: playing piano, playing office, dart baseball, photo-electric football, taking all the books off my mom's living room bookshelves and making long Childcraft tunnels with them, and writing death threats to my sister on pieces of paper that I left around the house for her to find. I only got to do that one day. "Dear Sister, you'll be dead soon. Your loving brother, Mike."

Sometimes the rain fell for ten days or even two weeks without let-up. Hearing a hard rain drumming on our shingled roof at night was one of the wonderful things about rain, consoling in its way as a good ghost story. Being in the attic right beside the warm, wallpapered chimney was about as comfortable as a kid could wish to get (notwithstanding Heidi's cozy loft in her grandfather's mountain cabin). One image I had of rain was someone sewing faster and faster on a treadle sewing machine, my mother's Singer.

Splashing in our galoshes through brown mud puddles on the way to school was always fun, and reaching the warm schoolhouse was the payoff for the journey. Of course, with rain, the playgrounds shut down which, in effect, "rained on our parade," but we had the so-called Little Gym and often got to play dodgeball, basketball, or wrestle on thick mats there.

Unfortunately, for recess, instead of running wild outside, we occasionally had to do orchestrated routines in the Little Gym, such as the "Hokey-pokey." The teachers took this so seriously, they actually would try to correct our movements as though we were training for the ballet. "You put your right foot in, you put your right foot out; you put your right foot in, and you shake it all about. You do the Hokey-Pokey, and you turn yourself around. That's what it's all about!" I couldn't imagine the moron who wrote that. Meanwhile-between 45-speed record changes, I would gaze longingly at the basketball hoop with the new white net at the far end of the gym.

Whenever we were in the Little Gym, you knew it must be raining. We loved the Little Gym, though. And the first time I kissed a girl that wasn't my mother or a woman relative was in the hallway of the balcony that overlooked the Little Gym and carried us from the grade school side of the school to the high school side. As you passed along the corridor you could look down through wire netting to the Little Gym below, where the kids were shouting (screaming, actually) and bouncing balls, playing games on the glossy hardwood floor (the net was to prevent us from throwing ourselves forty feet down into the gym in our eagerness to play, rather than to save us from our despair at having to return to the classroom).

I actually don't remember what girl I kissed, her identity having been forever erased from my fifth-grade brain by the repressive punishment that followed my affront, though I can assume that it had to be one of the desirables, say Tina, Marilyn, Mary, Judy, Patty, etc. It couldn't have been Patty II because she was too tall and it wasn't Hilda because she had ringworm and had to wear a scarf over her shaved head (she still looked rather cute, though, in a Middle Eastern sort of way).

There are some other possible *un*desirables, but it would be *un*gallant of me to even hint at their names here. Besides, I was told by older kids—and one even in high school—that many of the . . . how shall I put it . . . less beautiful girls in grade school by the time they get over their bumpy passage through teen-life often turn into butterflies, although some of the butterflies, by the time they leave high school and start life with pregnancies, factory work, or just a bum for a husband, prefer to have stayed in their cocoons.

I don't know what possessed me that day, but I had heard someone in class talking about having kissed someone and it recalled to me that little song, "Georgie Porgie Puddin' and Pie, who kissed a girl and made her cry." It sounded fun, and I was nothing if not suggestible. So out of the blue, between classes, I saw (let's say) either Marilyn or Tina, passing innocently, merrily along the corridor above the Little Gym (possibly even humming a little Christian hymn), coming in dimpled knees toward me, and I lurched out and pecked her on the lips.

I thought I'd done something rather liberated and making her cry was not my intention. I don't know if I made her cry or not, actually, because she just ran the other way like she'd been stung by a bee rather than kissed, and I didn't see her for a while because her homeroom was different than mine. Davy Lewis said she had been sent to Steilacoom, the nuthouse for girls, but I knew he was lying because Steilacoom was a nuthouse for adults. But my good-looking blonde fifth-grade teacher, Miss Larson, (whom my mom kidded—I think it was kidding—my dad about liking, what with Dad suddenly taking an interest in PTA and all) came to my desk and told me I'd have to stay after school (the victim of my advancements evidently may or may not have broken into tears, or been taken to the nuthouse, but Miss Larson was definitely talking to the authorities). Then to both my horror and secret pride, Miss Larson went in front of the class, and proceeded to denounce kissing in grade school in general and my conduct in particular.

"Mike knows what I'm talking about. Don't you, Mike?"

No, according to her, there wasn't going to be any such social experimentation, and she seemed to suggest that what I had done might encourage it, or at least spread the game of Post Office, a game not really understood by anyone I knew, but which had some unspoken tie to Valentine's Day. Miss Larson was putting her foot down on all of it right now, so I decided—with uncharacteristic petulance—to put my foot down on all of it as well, "No Valentine for you, Miss Larson," I declared to myself.

I might have expected Miss Larson's point of view from some of the older, more conservative teachers, but it was surprising coming from Miss Larson, no schoolmarm her. She was pretty and had blonde hair (I can't emphasize that enough), and we boys all thought her figure in her skirts was noteworthy, too. If we were, as they say, sweet on Miss Larson, it was our automatic nervous systems that were responsible.

On many rainy days, some of us would voluntarily stay after school and make board games, play twenty questions, or work on the class newspaper, our scandal sheet. Headline: Johnny Parsons Caught Picking His Nose in Class Again. Or: Billy James elected lavatory monitor for second term despite wanting to clean erasers. That wasn't the headline; that was the whole story. We never stayed voluntarily after school with any other teacher. I don't think we stayed after school to be with Miss Larson exactly, but to be in the warm environment she created by just being there at her desk grading papers or reading a book on education on rainy winter days. She was sunlight. She was 100 watts. Even though one side of her face had a little blemish, a slight pitting, I assume from the measles when she was a kid, we wanted her to enter the Miss Washington contest. Moms couldn't do that, but Miss Larson was an eligible bachelor. She laughed and blushed and said she wasn't pretty enough.

"You're the prettiest teacher in school and maybe in town," one of our Committee to Have Miss Larson Compete for Miss Washington said.

"Yeah, my Dad thinks so too," I added.

If she had been someone's mom, just think how she could help with homework. She was as pretty as my mom, but she had two advantages, that homework thing and the blondness. I really have to wonder if Miss Larson once in a while didn't feel a little uncomfortable with half a dozen of us boys hanging around after school to work on our projects. I'm just glad we didn't take up Davy Lewis's idea to follow her home from school. (We did invite her to come see our Fort once, "It's even got a dungeon!" but she declined, noting that the Fort was not on school property.

In and of itself that little peck on the mouth produced no significant remorse in me. After all, I'd kissed the girl, I hadn't hit her with a baseball bat, or put a dead frog in her lunch box, though my thoughts were drifting in that direction. To top things off, Miss Larson called my mother and thirty minutes into my detention (it was real detention because the sun was shining), my mother actually showed up at the classroom.

It's was very unusual and unsettling to see my mom in my classroom. (*Mothers in Your Classrooms*—now there's a horror movie for you.) And how odd I must have looked sitting alone in the middle of all the school desks at four o'clock when even the Wynooche Valley kids had left the playground, caught their buses, and gone home to farm chores. I felt odd, too.

After shaking off the shock of seeing my mother, I thought just maybe she had come to defend me, but she hardly gave me a glance. She and Miss Larson got into a long conversation sprinkled with laughter, but not even a smile for me. I was in hot water, as the saying goes, and the temperature was rising.

They must have chatted a full fifteen minutes. Maybe they were admiring each other's outfits. Maybe they had finally got around to discussing how my slight speech impediment had driven me to becoming an unnecessary talker, an idiosyncratic reader, a kid who'd do anything to get a laugh, or an equivalent amount of attention. And now, a kisser.

Finally, my mother escorted me to the car and we drove two blocks home. (She must have wanted to get to the school in a hurry to have driven there.) In the car, I can't remember what my mother said; I was scolded a little for my big crime, but my mother had had that long talk with Miss Larson and that seemed to have settled her down, for which I was grateful. I don't think I kissed anyone again until the seventh grade, when dancing with girls and kissing got to be practically *de rigueur.*

Well, I blame the rain for some, or all, of this and the hokey-pokey also. By the way, I think Davy Lewis from the other classroom got into the same trouble I did shortly afterward, despite the school-wide ban. So the song became "Davy Lewis Puddin' and Pie, kissed a girl and so did I." Sad to say, this ditty highly amused us. We were romantics. We were idiots.

Davy Lewis, by the way, probably deserved whatever detention he got just for his behavior at home. I always liked to trade comic books with Davy, as his collection was bigger than mine. Except for Scrooge McDuck, my favorite comics were the sordid ones. I still remember with a chill one of my favorites: A crazed husband wants to kill his wife, so he draws a bath for her, sprinkles in a packet of bubble bath, and a pint of acid, and invites her to get into the tub. The husband returns to the kitchen, fixes himself a tuna sandwich and a glass of milk, watches the news on television, and takes a nap. When he awakens and returns to the bathroom, all he finds is a gleaming skeleton (full color page) sitting in the tub.

Davy Lewis also used to charge his friends a nickel to look through the keyhole of the bathroom door at his younger sister taking a shower. I'm sure I must have taken a peek, but it was pretty dumb because the peephole only let you see a naked shoulder and his sister was so young she didn't even look completely like a girl yet.

Davy was also something of a practical joker. He liked to offer his friends nuts from a little paper bag. On crunching down on one, you found yourself eating garlic. He also had that rubber fake dog doo and fake vomit that he liked to leave on the carpets of friends he visited. In this, I was a cut above Davy, preferring to use the more elegant inkbottle-and-rubber-fake-ink spill.

But to return to rain (as it so religiously returned to us): It was like a god, a dark one, dictating most aspects of our lives until at last the sun won its way back to town. Although Grays Harbor had the distinction of having more cases of childhood rickets per capita than any U.S. county, it also surely had more books checked out from the library by kids than any other county.

And the rain, of course, made the world green for us and grew the biggest trees in the world! I don't know where all the birds went when it rained for weeks. I know where the ducks went; they took over the Elma golf course. But it all came down to this: I was lucky and grateful to live in a house with parents of reliable income, an older sister who was studious, books, and oil heat, and plenty of Mason jars of canned fruit in the basement. And there was no better way to endure the rains, the weeks of rain, the months of rain, and even in time to come to love what I came to call the Republic of Rain, than to be at home—or to be able to carry "home" around with you in the wet and stormy world when you weren't.

19 JIMMY & RANDY

I.

B EFORE MY CLASS of kids came along, the school administrators had been able to pack each grade (about thirty kids) into one schoolroom. When we came on board, another classroom was needed to stuff in another thirty. I was told it was because of World War II when all our fathers went off to fight the Japanese Empire and the Germans and some other misguided nations. And because our mothers got lonely in their absence, they, our mothers, decided to bring us kids into the world for company. But one thing was for sure: the doubled enrollment meant more children for our future ball teams. That was the important thing.

I can't write about every kid in my class, but I can mention a few who stood out. Take Randy Hopkins, for example. A good friend (and rival) who had so many talents you almost couldn't stand it. He could play piano, sing, dance, tumble, and top it all off with high grades. The girls liked him better than they seemed to like any of the rest of us (I'm not sure they even liked the rest of us), and Randy was always welcome at our sandlot football games because he was a good lineman, a fairly big lineman who didn't need to carry the ball all the time to enjoy himself. The girls didn't just like him, by the way; he actually liked them.

He was our doctor's son and lived in the biggest new house in town, which included a school-like drinking fountain when you first came in the backdoor, and a sunken living room with thick wall-to-wall carpeting—the most perfect playing field imaginable for marble games on rainy days.

Every year, Randy's father, Doc, went to Detroit and drove back home in a new Cadillac. My mom said he deserved such a car because he always came to our house when we were sick and to other people's when they were out of sorts as well. She said the town, and especially sick people, really liked Doc Hopkins' bedside manner, and they, she said, were the ones who bought him that car every year.

Let me comment on that bedside manner. When I had to have a shot, usually for stepping on a nail while working on the Fort, I could take it like a man just so long as my mother held my hand and I could look away from the place where Doc stabbed me. In time, I didn't need my hand held anymore, but I still had to look away from the point of injection. But my disassociation from pain took a decided step backward when Doc Hopkins came to our house to inject both my sister and me who were suffering from chicken pox. These shots were to be given in one cheek or the other of our bottoms, and being the good brother, I told my sister she could go first. I was supposed to leave the room while the first shot was administered, but I made the mistake of peeking around the door only to see Doc Hopkins transformed into a bloodthirsty MD, who, after loading up the needle with venom, raised his arm and needle high over his head, and stabbed it downward into my sister's tiny behind.

"Your turn, Mike," my mother called as I was heading for the backdoor.

My turn, forget it. I was down the hall in my pajamas and out on the porch when Mom caught up to me.

"Hey, now. Where do you think you're going?"

"I saw everything," I told her. "I saw everything," I gasped.

Then Doc Hopkins appeared at the back door, looking large but more normal now.

"What's wrong, Shirley?" He asked.

"Oh, I think Mike saw you give Sharon the shot."

"You've got to have one as well, Mike. You don't want your sister getting well and you having to stay in bed."

That was reasonable. "Okay, but I want the shot in my arm."

"It will make your arm a lot sorer than if I give it in your hind-quarters."

"Arm." I said.

"Bee-hind." Doc said.

"Mom?"

"Bee-hind." She said.

We often spent Christmas Eve at the Hopkins' home. Dad and Doc, after having a few rum eggnogs, tried one year to assemble a bicycle intended for a present for Judy, one of Randy's three sisters. They had a heck of a good time putting it together, and when they had finished, no test pilot in the world would have dared to ride it. In fact, it looked like the one-man band machine of the Sheriff Tex kid show, all horns and washboards, drums, and whistles. Maybe Dad and Doc needed more eggnog.

A less humorous memory was the time Randy's multi-talented personality was getting on my nerves a little. We were playing basketball at Jimmy's driveway near the courthouse, and a little streak of meanness got into me. Maybe my team was losing or I was just passing through a phase when I was feeling the effects of the aggressive gene inherited from the top of the O'Connor family tree, a tree whose top was loaded with Irish warrior-kings.

That day I was actually laying, as they say, for Randy. At some point between games, I picked a fight with him and before I had done anything but attack him, he had me in a stranglehold that was choking the nonsense out of me. Finally, as I was turning blue in the face, he released me, got hurriedly on his bicycle, and rode home. Perhaps, he had choked me a little harder than necessary, but I certainly had something like it coming. But things really went bad when Randy went home and told his mother, Evelyn, and his mother called up Jimmy's mom, Gladis, who called me in from the driveway ball court and said Randy's mom wanted to speak to me on the telephone, and Randy's mom told me to come up to Doc's house because she wanted to talk to me, and I went up, and she scolded me good, and then I went home and told a slightly different version of events to my mother, and she, in a huff, called up Doc's wife and told her she shouldn't have interfered the way she did, and then and then . . . Just a little stupid kid's fight, and the whole town was sliding into civil war. I can't remember ever laying for anyone after that, but the Randy Chokehold I adopted for defense.

It was the Hopkin's family that was first in our town to have a collection of 45-speed records of radio bloopers. I think they were played at social functions that Doc and his wife held at their home. It wasn't long, though, before Randy had Jimmy Dockers and me up to his house to hear them on our own. They were pretty funny, and because they were intended for adults only, they were even funnier being in our hands. Two examples have remained with me. The first had a radio announcer commenting when he thought he was off the air. A lady soprano singer hit a note so high and shrill, the announcer blurted out, "Who goosed the soprano?!" We loved that one. The second was the wife of a professional golfer who told an interviewer she always kissed the balls of her husband before he played in a tournament. We played the blooper records again and again.

There was a new girl in town, named Cathy Cedar, who was assigned the seat right to my left in our sixth grade class. I already had a good friend named Tina Herrick on my right, and although Tina and I weren't, how shall I say, involved, Tina provided me sufficient distraction, considering I already had a girlfriend, Patti Havens, a year behind me in Mr. Ottoman's fifth-grade class.

Cathi Cedar, being new to town, imprinted on me fast. I talked to her in whispers from my desk whenever she started a conversation, usually as soon as Mr. Clemens, our teacher, was writing something on the board with his back to us. I did like Cathi; she was good looking and had the beginnings of little breasts. But there was something strangely older about her, and she had more freckles on her face than seemed the norm.

It wasn't too long before she invited some of our class to a dance party to be held at her house. I knew she wanted me to come and I really wanted to go, but my mother said sixth grade was still too young for dance parties. I wasn't *that* crazy about going and dancing with Cathi Cedar, so I probably shot hoops at the church gym that day or rode my bike over to Paul's for a game of Monopoly. But Randy Hopkins went and I assume danced up a little storm with Cathi. I don't know for sure, but what I do know is that darn soon afterwards, Randy and Cathi were going steady.

Trying to put the best face on things, I even thought that maybe Randy's dad, Doc, might be able to remove some of Cathi's excessive freckles some night after they had a big social event at the Doc's house and after they had laughed themselves silly playing 45-speed blooper records. I'm also sure, once Cathi was introduced to the riches of the family with the new Cadillac and all, she'd want to be hanging around that indoor drinking fountain.

It's so strange, all of this, because while I liked the new girl Cathi Cedar, I really had stopped short of wanting her to replace my girlfriend Patti in the fifth grade. I was already starting to like younger girls rather than older ones and Cathi Cedar seemed like she belonged in High School. Then one night at the movie house, Friday night of course, I came face to face with jealousy, the Red-Eyed Monster. There in the wings of the theater were Randy and Cathi and they weren't just holding hands or touching shoulders. No, Randy had actually taken off his big winter coat and put it over his and Cathi's head. They were snuggled under his coat in an improvised tent and maybe even *kissing*.

This all made a big stir among the Friday night movie kids, or so I imagined. No one could keep their eyes on the movie so intent was everyone to watch the goings on of the lovebirds. I admit Randy's inventive technique was in advance of mine; I had been trying just to get up enough moxie to sit with a girl in the movies, to do enough of the right and pleasing things to keep a girl seated beside me through the cartoons. And I had no logical reason to be jealous of Randy since I'd kind of had first choice on Cathi Cedar and passed it up. I thought of putting in a transfer with Mr. Clemens for a seat change, thinking it was going to be hard to sit through class beside Cathi Cedar without thinking about throwing a coat over her head, but Cathi tended to whisper to me less and less and I actually did much better in math.

Several months after this, I met my girlfriend Patti at a Sunday movie matinee and because there was hardly anybody in the theater, we decided to duck under the red velvet cord that guarded the stairs to the balcony and take two back seats up there. I thought about Randy's coat routine, even though I was just wearing a light jacket. When I struggled to take it off while seated with a big bag of popcorn between my legs I smacked Patti in the jaw with my arm. "What are you doing?" she blurted out. "Patti," I said, "I don't actually know."

II.

"Neat" was the way I'd describe Jimmy Dockers. A short blonde kid who most of us, though we never spoke of it, only felt it, so maybe it wasn't all of us who recognized it, but I know I did, recognize, that is, Jimmy's special qualities. There was something in his person and in most of what he did that was luminous, finer in form than anyone else. When we played basketball, usually at the driveway of his house behind the courthouse on Spruce Street, great spirited games were played, and although Jimmy did about everything on the court like the rest of us mortals, he could take a hook shot from deep in the right forward corner (near the steps to his back porch) and make it. All net.

It was sweet to see especially if he was on your team, and devastating if he wasn't, though still deserving of applause. Well, the hook shot was one thing. When we played football, Jimmy, at halfback, wasn't nearly as evasive as I was. I could run fast, but even better, maneuver around opposing tacklers like a bat, as if the tacklers had been instructed *not* to tackle me. But Jimmy liked to do something I didn't like to do at all, namely, dive like a full-grown pro halfback smack into the line.

He had such a compact way of holding his body together as he plunged into the line, well aware that he'd only make a yard or two, that his failure to gain much wasn't of consequence. It was fearless football (like that hook shot he gambled to take) and so free of self. I really liked tackling him also, as though he ran partly to satisfy our joy of crunching someone his own size. But he could scamper and when he did break through a hole in the line, he would run like his crewcut was on fire.

I liked to have Jimmy on my team, but I also liked tackling him so much, I didn't mind playing against him. Now someone like red-haired Terry Ratchet, well, he was good to have on your team because for one thing he was a year older and for another he had a kind of angry way of running and being tackled. (I've later come to think his style, or lack of it, relates, perhaps, to what is called "class war.") He wasn't fun to down because of his bony elbows, and when you tackled him somewhere near the sideline, afterwards you felt mugged.

Pete Baylor, an even older friend, was harder to tackle because he was bigger, but he wasn't a major threat because he was slow, and though it'd take two of us at least to bring him down, we would have had enough time to place an announcement in the *Montesano Vidette* asking for tacklers, and they would have had time to put on their sweats, answer the ad, and still make the tackle on Pete.

Little Johnny Rachet was fast and younger, but he didn't go plunging into the line like Jimmy and you'd best get to him before he skirted the end or you'd be chasing his tennis shoes to pay dirt. Bobby was fun to tackle also and to knock out of bounds.

While I'm on this line of characterization, I should mention that there was always a kid like Andrew Fortner who played very well while his team was ahead, but always got hurt when his team was behind. I wasn't the greatest sport myself, I hated losing, though I always preferred to be on a physically weaker team over a team of stronger athletes, loving the challenge, the esprit de corps and the upset. But I wasn't someone who took losing graciously.

It was Jimmy I remember for his class. Off the field, he practiced the piano each evening, and he had already earned a number of those white plaster busts of composers that he placed on the top of his piano and which guarded over him as he practiced Baroque or Classical pieces in the living room.

Jimmy was also a first-rate student and mostly got A's in every subject. When I entered the first grade, the grade was divided for the first time into two classes because our generation of war babies was swelling the census, as I mentioned above. That's why my friendship with Jimmy took so long to mature; we never ended up in the same class though we were always in the same grade. What brought us most closely together, however, were the sports leagues we created with card games, marble games, and photo-electric games, through which we developed mirror images of the Big Leagues. During the rainiest of days, we'd spend hours together or apart playing the various sports games and keeping meticulous statistics of each batter, runner, and play.

For one marble game of baseball, I built out of wood scraps a three-deck stadium about four-feet high to put outside the outfield wall of my miniature ballpark. I used an empty box of Quaker Oats to pitch a marble against, and the marble would bounce out into the field where other marbles standing in for position players would make moves (with my assistance) to throw the runner out. If I hit a sweet spot on the Quaker Oats box with a marble, it would fly up over the two-by-four outfield fence which had ads pasted on them. When I built the three-story stadium, I decided I needed fans to sit in it, and so I drilled what seemed a million shallow holes that I filled with individual marbles to the number of some three hundred. (Believe it or not, I had names for a great number of the marbles, many of which I was on a personal basis with.)

Getting ready for a ball game you can imagine took a lot of time: situating the fences, measuring off the right distance for placement of the bases, and seating all the marble-fans. Because the floors of the stadium slanted inward (a structural flaw), if a marble was dislodged from the front row, it dislodged a whole bunch more before the throng came to rest at the back of the stadium, where, unluckily for them, no one was selling hotdogs or soda pop. All filled up, though, the stadium looked impressive. "It's a capacity crowd, ladies and gentleman," I'd be broadcasting, " and the first batter is . . ."

Pretty soon my mother suggested I take the stadium and the game outdoors, because it was getting quite impossible to put up the fences, fill the stadium, and take it all down in the living room in a day. Also Mom was getting tired of sucking up marbles in her Hoover vacuum cleaner. We found our cat one morning actually asleep on the top deck of the stadium and about a zillion marble-fans had fallen out of their seats to their deaths on the floor, some, who'd rolled under the sofa, inevitably on their way to Hoover Heaven.

When I moved the stadium outside, it wasn't long before I had the grass worn down smooth so the marbles would roll clean. I'd run a game a day when the weather was right, and pretty soon Terry Ratchet, who was so good with tools, had built a bigger and niftier stadium in his backyard, though when fall came, his logger father made him chop it up for kindling.

Another kid, Gene Austen, who seldom played real baseball, surprised everyone by building with his little sister a stadium across town. We rode our bikes over to see it and it was pretty clever, especially because he'd glued all the marbles into the holes. "These, "he said, "are the permanent seats."

Then Jimmy joined the action and built, as you might guess, a smaller but very trim and neat stadium with a tiny press box that he could use strictly indoors. It was an all-weather stadium with painted cardboard figures (rather than marbles) pasted into the levels of the stadium. I don't know if any other stadiums were constructed that summer, but I do know it was the seasonal craze. I left mine outside into September when the big rains came and discolored it. I wanted to save it for the next season, but that hope faded in the same way colors on some of my shirts faded when my mom used too much bleach to get out grass stains. When the little field and the stadium began to be covered first by red and yellow maple and pear leaves, then soggy black ones, I carried a burlap sack out to the field and took all the wet spectators out of the stadium and put them in the sack. I didn't mind closing down the ballpark, but I didn't want to lose all my marbles.

20 SUNDAY

Sunday mornings in Montesano always dawned with bird-song and cloudless skies—the ideal play weather. But no time to even read the Funnies, got to put on those dark scratchy wool pants, starched white shirt, and stiff black shoes, and walk with the family up Sylvia Street—one corner to the next—to St. Mark's Episcopal Church. It was, however, a blessing that the church was so close—it saved a little extra time for play.

At a very early age I had sincere appreciation of what I felt to be God, but I confess I never had much religious feeling at church or Sunday school. BE GOOD! I got that much. But, for example, those comic book pictures of Jesus and other Bible figures in Sunday school didn't inspire me. The comic books—thinner for some reason than the standard 10-cent kind available at the drug store—were virtually un-tradable.

"Hey, Davy, I've brought you a really keen comic of old Moses. Look here, he's going right up that rugged mountain all by himself to talk to God!"

"Bible comics don't cut it," said Davy, wearing a green eye shade like a bookie and surrounded in his upstairs room by tall stacks of comic books. "Too doctrinaire."

I'd slide into one of the pews, or high-backed benches, and wait for the show to begin. It was uncomfortable right from the get-go—my wool pants itching and my starched shirt collar choking me. The stained glass windows depicted vaguely similar bible scenes that our

Sunday school comics did, but the windows, while colorful, blocked the light and a view of the trees. It was strange in there. Once the congregation was seated, I usually couldn't see anything in front of me because all the women wore hats and some of the hats, I swear, were three feet tall if you counted the tips of the feathers.

At some point the organ and the choir, which I couldn't see, being too short, would start and everyone would stand up and sing along. I'd had enough piano lessons to know that something was off several keys here and that if it wasn't for the lead in the stained glass the next hymn, or the next, could break every sacred window in the place.

To kneel on the long footstool in front of me for any length of time was a painful exercise. Dropping down on to it was like dropping into a rabbit burrow. Staying on it was even worse than sitting in a chair facing the corner of the room at school. The church furniture was designed without a thought to children; just like the Bible, I figured, as well as its teaching of original sin, a teaching, though, that I concluded absolved kids of the responsibility for everything wrong they did. "I'm sorry, Mrs. Thomkins we broke your window with our baseball. It's just that niggling original sin of ours."

After something like thirty minutes standing and sitting, but mostly kneeling, each new prayer found me clinging desperately to the bench in front of me like a man lost at sea clinging to a broken beam of shipwreck. My knees shook and I sweated profusely. At last, thank heavens, the sermon arrived, which we didn't have to kneel through and were free rather to squirm through.

Just to indicate the special place of church in children's lives, note that kids play house, play bank, play cowboys and Indians, play office, play school, play store, but, to my knowledge, seldom church. The sermon from the pulpit always dragged on and on, however, like a doubleheader, between two teams in the cellar in September, minor league teams. I don't honestly remember a word of any of the hundreds I sat through. But then I wasn't confirmed. My mother always seemed to listen seriously, but my father, well, it was hard to tell because he had on his Department of Agriculture face, attentive but giving nothing away. My sister, seated on the other side of Dad, however, had the rapt and shining face of Joan of Arc.

When the sermon ended, no one ever applauded, which was fitting in one way but impolitic to my schooled sense of things. Then Father Frank, like an army lieutenant calling in an air strike, would announce a hymn number and the congregation would rise and start a new attack of singing.

Finally, everyone went up to the wooden railing around the candle-lit altar to take Communion, except me and other unconfirmed kids (we were confirmed kids, just not yet confirmed Episcopalians); we could just suffer there in the pews without food or drink. An acolyte kid working the aisle with a big golden platter followed Communion. The platter was passed down each pew like a relay game, and when the platter came to you, you put money, or envelopes with money, onto it. By the time it reached the back rows of the church, it was necessary to introduce a second platter to hold all the loot. Then the platters were brought back to the altar and Father Frank, who, without counting the take, but quickly sizing it up, held the golden platters up to the cross and sang a short prayer of thanks (as I would have done in his place). Then another acolyte whisked the money off stage into the wings (where maybe Father Frank's wife was waiting to count it).

We all sang one or two more hymns while the procession of choir members and acolytes formed and then passed down the aisle. Father Frank came last, Bible in hand, singing his heart out. Feeling my first wave of Sunday spirituality, itchy to be out of there, I'd think it was over; but it wasn't quite.

At the church door, there'd always be a big bottleneck where Father Frank was greeting the parishioners one by one. Finally my mother would put her arm around my shoulders on the sunlit porch (of course clouds had begun rolling in from the west by now, threatening the chances of outdoor play) and Father Frank would bend over me to shake my well-scrubbed hand, saying, "It's good to see you, Michael. How are you today."

"I'm fine, thank you, Father."

"He's a nice boy, Shirley," he'd say to my Mother. Then to my father, "And Tom, thanks again for your work on the new building. You parishioners did a wonderful job."

Then back to me: "How's the playhouse going?"

This was a reference to our Fort. In negotiating for the salvage wood from the old church, we had been careful to say it was for a playhouse, not a three-story fort with a dungeon and gun slits.

(I had called the Fort a shack when I first asked Father Frank about using the old church wood to build it. But I shifted ground real fast when he said, "Come again?")

"We want to build a playhouse," I said. "All the kids in the neighborhood want to build a playhouse." Then we began hauling the wood like ants from the corner of Spruce and Sylvia, behind the odd single-story apartment complex with four little units for people without real homes or real families and across the alley lined with maple trees to the backyard of our house on the corner of Sylvia Street and Broadway.

When kids would ask what we were building, we'd say "a fort"; when parents asked: "a clubhouse"; when Father Frank came round: "a playhouse"; but we hated that kindergarten word so much that we were tempted on occasion to come right out with the truth: "It's really a fort, Father Frank. For war."

But because Protestants, unlike Catholics, don't have to confess themselves to a priest, I never had to tell Father Frank that his old church had become in its second life a fort. (Thinking about this now, it doesn't seem a very big deal one way or the other. But I wasn't thinking about this that way then.)

109

"It's three floors now, thank you, Father. But it doesn't have any stained windows like yours. We could also use some more nails."

This amused him. "Well, someday maybe you can build a church like this one."

I was about to reply, but at that moment Father Frank turned his attention to another family that had crowded into the spotlight.

With church over and gray clouds streaming ever faster above the broadleaf maples on Sylvia Street, our family walked home. As soon as I got to our house, I kicked off the shiny shoes, jumped out of my scratchy pants (checking briefly to see if I was bleeding), and removed the white shirt. With a wave of a wand, so to speak, I was back in my patched jeans (with rabbit foot chained to belt loop), sweatshirt, tennis shoes, and ball cap. I dodged something my Mother was calling out from the kitchen and was outside at last in the backyard fresh air. Unfortunately, all the neighbor kids were still untangling themselves from Sunday church, so I was alone out there with Carolina, my dog, and the Fort, with the wind rising and the sky getting darker and darker.

21 MARY AT THE MOVIES

MARY STEPHENS AND I had been exchanging smiles in our class-room for a couple months. They were often smiles like inside jokes, communicating our sharing an understanding of something amusing to us going on in the classroom, for instance, when some-one got caught by the teacher sticking gum under their seat, passing notes, or getting an easy question completely wrong. Smile, smile. It happened by accident, this discovery of one another across three rows of classmates, but it turned into a conspiracy and finally a lik-ing; that would be "liking," in quotes or italics.

"Do you like Mary?" Donna Wakoski, Mary's best friend, asked me in the hall on my way to the drinking fountain.

"Yes. I think I do. Yes."

"Too bad. She doesn't like you," Donna said.

"Then I don't like her."

"I'm just kidding. She really likes you."

"I like her too."

"She hates you, ha, ha."

"She hates me?"

"But I like you."

"Huh?"

"Hey, I'm only kidding. Does David like me?"

"David who?"

"David Gowen, whose dad owns the candy store."

"Oh, that David."

"Does he like me?"

"I don't know."

"Mary hates you."

Mary and I continued our connection for quite a while, and I became for the first time in my life attached to a smile from a girl who was not a relation. And a beautiful girl at that. Exchanging smiles with her was even better than a blue sky (sort of), and considering Grays Harbor weather, that was saying a lot, saying a lot because in Grays Harbor we didn't get enough vitamin D from sunshine and that caused periodic rickets epidemics.

On the few occasions when Mary didn't return a smile, I'd feel my heart sinking faster than one of my bathtub Battle Creek Michigan plastic submarines filled with baking powder. No one had prepared me for the dark side of this liking business.

I came to know everything she wore, from her black shoes and white socks to the different colored ribbons tied in her hair. She was a brunette, not a blonde (somehow I'd always thought I'd fall for a blonde, hopefully one with a pony tail), and she had a little mole above her lip, very smooth skin, and her eyes were soft brown and the color of her hair.

Her skin (I was even contemplating her skin!) was very fair. She sat closer to the front of the class than I did, so I could look at her without her noticing. And it was strange how I could feel so interested in doing just that, looking at her in a way I had no interest to look at anyone else in the whole school. I got satisfaction out of looking at her, but it could actually make me a little dizzy, and becoming dizzy, I could scare myself into thinking I was losing my mind. I liked watching snow fall and clouds drift away; I liked watching the Dodgers in the World Series on TV; I liked looking on Montesano from the south side swamps and at Sylvia Lake's silver surface through the trees just before we descended to the bridge that spanned it; I liked seeing all kinds of things, but looking at Mary was the best.

At some point I knew somehow (probably from watching older boys in the movie house balcony) it was time to advance our relationship; and my plan was to sit with her at the movies. (I would gladly have walked her home, but Mary rode the school bus—I wasn't that desperate, yet.) One Friday night—the night the adults never go to the movies, or if they do, they don't stay long—I saw Mary sitting in the front row of the theater with her friend Donna. I steeled my nerves, as they say, and strode boldly down the aisle and scooted into the seat beside her. Mary didn't say a word or look at me. She just sat there craning her cute neck up at the screen and eating popcorn in small portions with her right hand, which was familiar to me from her raising it often in class. Donna on the other side of Mary did say something to Mary and glanced from behind Mary's popcorn bag at me.

I figured I was safe so far.

The movie screen was so close and loud (I preferred sitting far back) that it was hard to concentrate on my next move. Suddenly and inexplicably I found myself thinking about Donna. We shared a couple attributes: pigeon toes and a slight lisp. When I first read what a Gypsy was, I thought of Donna. But she was an unreliable go-between. Donna wasn't Mary, but she was worth a look now and then.

The movie roared and thundered as the three of us sat there with our heads thrown back like astronauts. We had watched a good deal of the film when a buzzer went off in my imagination. It was time to put my arm around Mary, or on the back of her chair, to be precise. My elbow went into action first. I kept it close to my body as it pulled the arm and hand into a position level with the back of Mary's chair. Then the arm (now working independent of me) began to slide snake-like across the back of her seat. If I had been her, the whole business would have scared the daylights out of me. Finally the arm got stretched out fully and rested on her seat

113

in contact with a little bit of her hair. I didn't move. Mary didn't move either. I was afraid to breathe.

We three astronauts continued traveling through the black and white noisy universe. Soon, though, I realized my arm was too high and over-extended. It was beginning to hurt to keep it there. But I didn't dare risk a big adjustment; I was where I'd thought I was going to be happy. I couldn't back off now.

The movie had lots of car chases and gunplay; someone had just robbed a bank and was racing toward a steel drawbridge, but the bridge was slowly opening for a tall-masted boat. In addition to my arm—now more numb than hurting—a terrible crick was developing in my neck. I couldn't really move my arm or my head. I was beginning to feel like a pretzel. Meanwhile, Mary was—rather annoyingly—still calmly working on her popcorn. She reminded me for a terrifying moment of my sister, who could make a bag of popcorn and a box of Juji Fruits last through a double feature, while I was lucky to have anything left after the previews, or even before the previews had concluded.

When the movie ended—unmercifully for the bad guys, but mercifully for me, the human pretzel—Donna and Mary got up from their seats and began scooting out the row the other way from me. Mary paused, though, and looked back at me—was it a look of pity or of utter bafflement?—and then said something to Donna and left.

It was the only time in my life I ever stayed in the theater and watched the movie credits. It was a small cast, but oddly they thanked the city for using its drawbridge. And I thanked my lucky stars that my arm—still pinned to Mary's vacated seat—wasn't my pitching arm.

Finally, the previews started again and an usher with a big flashlight came down the aisle and told me I had to leave, or buy another ticket. I managed to pry my arm from the back of the seat, lower gingerly my cricked neck, and trod the long uphill, carpeted aisle to the bright lights of concession land. Everyone there was buying movie treats, popcorn, candy—happy to be about to see a stupid movie (and probably to do a lot of snuggling).

Once out onto the dark and drizzly streets of downtown Montesano, I felt like I needed to find one of those bars they have in the movies for lonely guys. I needed a drink and a big cigarette. I was getting wet and it was still three and a half blocks to my house, but I skipped the bar this time and headed home. The rain, though, I discovered, made me feel tougher.

22 THE INDIA MOVIE

JUST THE MOST haunting movie I ever saw wasn't even at our downtown movie house on Second Street. It was a documentary shown at school to our fifth grade class in our little library. Everyone—teachers included—was starved for something more entertaining than a film on nutrition or bicycle safety. For several years now, however, we at least hadn't had to suffer further Civil Defense films; the bomb was still a threat, I assume, but as fifth graders, it was getting harder to fit, with ease or celerity, under our desks to practice anti-radiation or preventive bomb-blinding tactics. This far along in our collective growing process, there was even, for example, one big classmate, Dexter, our champion wrestler, who could hardly fit *into* his desk, let alone *under* it. If an atomic bomb—heaven forbid!—should drop on the school, I guess the Civil Defense people weren't concerned about big kids like Dexter, but I also couldn't figure why they would favor—as their safety drill seemed to do—short, agile, and talkative kids like me. We were mostly learning to live with the bomb by ignoring it, which we found harder to do with regard to the white crosses springing up along Highway 101 to mark where people died in automobile crashes. Going to the moon, however, that idea, by contrast to destruction in a mushroom cloud, we kept expectantly alive.

Like all documentaries it was in black & white and didn't run long enough to fill a whole class hour. The subject was death and fertility, a snake cult. It began by taking us to a small village in India. I don't remember the name of the village, or the name of the movie, or the name of the characters (I didn't remember who I was while I was watching the movie either, as you'll see why). I do remember, though, that it was early in the year in this village and there was a festival going on to celebrate the return of spring. (I could say it was like our May festival, the winding of the maypole, the crowning of the king and queen of the May, etc., but it wasn't.)

Each spring festival the elders in big beards and white flowing robes walk through the unpaved tiny village and knock on the door of a family who has a young virgin. How they select which virgin, I'm clueless, but something tells me it wasn't the way our class selected our eraser cleaner or lavatory monitor. The one they picked had long black hair, dark skin, and big dark eyes and, in her white robe, she was very pretty, but quite different pretty from Montesano girls who usually were more cute than pretty, though that was probably because they were still so young, and once, they became virgins, I then assumed, they might be just as pretty as the India girl.

The elders in their beards and robes led the girl out of the village and into the hills. Hundreds of villagers (that would be pretty much the whole village) and a few scrawny dogs followed the elders and the virgin up the winding dirt road into the hills, which had no trees or road signs.

Finally the entourage, deep in the hills now, left the road and followed a path to a clearing just below the face of a barren cliff. The elders performed a number of ceremonies with bells and incense, and several lotus flowers were placed in the girl's long black hair.

Now the drama heated up. One of the elders began blowing on a strange-shaped horn, a conch, the narrator called it. He walked to the face of the cliff and blew directly into what was the opening of a small cave. He blew and he blew and we thought he was trying to blow the cliff down like the wolf in "The Three Little Pigs." Another elder took over and blew and blew into the mouth of the cave. Then it appeared: A long ugly king cobra! It slid out of the cave, arched up, and struck at the horn-blowing bearded elder. The bearded elder almost fell over backward and quickly scampered to safety. The snake also startled us who were there in the dark in the library in Montesano riveted to the screen.

The narrator informed us that now the virgin princess would take over the situation. It was up to her to kiss (we couldn't believe this when we heard it), yes kiss, the cobra three times on its head, presumably without being kissed backed. "It is very dangerous," said the narrator gravely. (Tell us about it.)

The girl began singing and circling the cobra. I noticed she had a jingling anklet and was in bare feet rather than tennis shoes, and was dancing. The snake would rear up and strike at her, but like a prizefighter (sort of) she always managed to dodge the blows. Then, catching the snake off guard (and us watching), she rushed a few steps forward and kissed the top of the head of the cobra. The cobra spit poison and you could see her robe getting stained with the venom. She did this twice more and then walked away from the snake in triumph (and, we imagined, some relief).

The villagers were elated and threw flowers at the virgin and lifted her onto their shoulders and carried her back down to the village. Boy, what a show. We didn't need popcorn or Milk Duds to enjoy it.

But it's odd. I don't know how this film related to our studies at the time. I have a suspicion that in small schools out West like ours, a lot of movies got circulated just because our teachers had to have something novel once in a while to show us. It was educational and memorably disturbing. I mean I loved the film, but judging from our teacher's reaction, I don't think he had any more idea what the film was about before seeing it than we did. Immediately after seeing this film, I suspected that among the girls in our fifth grade, not many would ever want to become virgins, at least not if they were traveling to India in the springtime.

I recall Brenda Pearson's comment to Donna Wakoski while our class was funneling out of the library and back to the daylight of our homeroom. She said the girl in the movie looked a little like Donna. Donna was the darkest-skinned girl in our class whom I'd nicknamed privately Gypsy. And Brenda was right. Then Brenda giggled and said she didn't really like the movie. The snake had disappointed her. This caught my ear because if anything the snake had played its part fiercely and convincingly.

"I thought when the girl kissed the snake . . . how many times?"

"Three," said Gypsy.

"Yes, three," repeated Brenda. "I thought when the girl kissed the snake it would turn into a prince. I was quite disappointed."

23 LORD OF THE PEACOCKS

O N SUNDAY AFTERNOONS we sometimes drove to Olympia, the capital of our state, to visit my non-farm Grandfather and Grandmother. We had a comfortable two-door Ford then, and it would take us about an hour on Highway 101 to get there. Along the way, my sister and I in the back seat would always try to coax my father into stopping at the top of the hill on the way out of Mcleary (home of a wooden-door-making plant and the Bear Festival) at a store that sold chocolate-covered ice cream bars. Sometimes he'd stop but most times he wouldn't because we were only half an hour from plenty of sweets at Grandma's.

We had more success getting him to stop at the popcorn trucks at the foot of the big hill in Tacoma—where my sister was born and my great grandfather long ago built a factory to manufacture boilers—just after we had passed under a series of grey concrete overpasses and played the game of "Duck or Get Your Head Cut Off." The difference was that going through Tacoma meant we were on a much longer journey to my farm grandmother who lived near the Canadian border, and, consequently were hours from her always-filled cookie jar.

There was a pretty stretch of trees west of Olympia along both sides of the highway, and when we got to it my dad always asked us to name the various species, which I never could do nor could my sister or my mom very adequately. I knew my fir trees because we had an old pitchy one in our yard, and I knew my apple, pear, cherry, and plum trees thanks to their fruit.

After the customary tree quiz (it was only after my sister actually could name all the trees she was asked that I took the exercise seriously and began a study of the names of the Northwest ones), my sister went on to learn all the names (Latin and common) of the wild flowers as well, which was pretty show-offy by my reckoning, so I decided to know all the makes of the cars on the highway.

"What make was that blue car?"

"I don't know."

How about the red one that just passed us?

"I don't know and I don't care."

"What's the make and model of the car we're riding in?

"Would you move over to your side of the seat, please?!

Often when we arrived in Olympia, we'd go with my grandparents to a park or beach for a picnic. I especially liked Priest Point Park in north Olympia. The park, on the edge of South Puget Sound, where some mothballed black and red World War II battleships were anchored, had many picnic sites with tables, a big baseball field with a tall backstop, and real bases. And it had peacocks, which wandered freely through the park woods and grounds.

Those exotic birds were not only interesting and beautiful, but they always afforded an opportunity for my Dad to demonstrate some of his animal husbandry. We'd be gathered at the picnic table eating potato salad, hot dogs, and watermelon, when one of the peacocks, long tail swaying, would approach us. They were tame and unafraid of humans, and they seemed to know better than to venture onto the baseball diamond or the horseshoe pits.

We'd be eating and talking and one of the birds would come our way, perhaps expecting to share in our picnic, and Dad would get up from the table and start talking gently to it about one thing or another, and then suddenly grab it.

Before the peacock could cry out its piercing alarm, Dad would tuck its head under a wing and begin rocking it back and forth like it was a parcel post package. Pretty soon he'd leave off rocking the bird and set it gently down on the grass. The bird, now asleep, would stay exactly in the same position Dad had set it down in.

Other peacocks would wander near our picnic table, drawn I guess by their curiosity about their sleeping bird of a feather. Dad would repeat the process, and soon, there would be three or maybe four peacocks slumbering on the grass around our picnic table. Picnickers nearby sometimes ambled over to our table wondering about the immobilized birds. But Dad wasn't showing off to the general public; he was showing off to us kids and my mother. My grandmother didn't like the demonstration but my grandfather was highly supportive. "Here, Tom, put this one to sleep."

My mother in her way was not thrilled about making a spectacle either. "Tom, for gosh sakes, wake the birds up. We don't want the Park authorities coming over here."

"Oh, they'll wake up soon enough," my father would say, putting his pipe in the corner of his mouth with satisfaction. "I do this all the time with chickens; it doesn't hurt them."

Dad was also sometimes the poultry judge at the county fair. He surely knew he wasn't hurting the peacocks because he liked poultry a lot. Though I later learned he often told farmers which chickens had to be culled, that is to say, which chickens had to have their heads cut off to keep a flock healthy and productive.

We ate lots of chicken at our house, of course, and I was beyond childhood before I ever figured out that all the birds in my Grandmother's chicken coop near Canada eventually were like those we ate at home. It's one of those realities you don't want to know about until you're big enough to handle it or rationalize it.

My Dad's trick with the peacocks impressed me. I'd leave off wolfing down a hot dog (another area to eventually address) and go over to one of the sleeping peacocks.

"Don't touch them," my mom would warn, "they have mites."

So I'd circle around them until sure enough one would suddenly pull its head out from its wing, spring to its feet, shake all its feathers, and strut away in full pride.

Soon another would awaken and so on until they were all up on their feet, shaking themselves and strutting away (wondering, I imagine, what had hit them). They reminded me of large flowers bursting into bloom.

Overall, in spite of being my father, Dad was a pretty amusing fellow. (Grandma once called him a bit of a rake.) Whenever we might be traveling with him—to Aberdeen, Bellingham, Olympia, or Seattle—and we were waiting for some reason for Mother to come back to our car, just my sister and I with Dad in the Ford, Dad might, to pass the time and to amuse us, start putting thoughts into the minds of passing pedestrians.

I can't remember word-for-word any of the comments, but they were rather impolite to the passers-by (if they had heard), which is what made them so funny and kept my sister and me laughing and entertained waiting for Mother to come back from shopping or an errand. This kind of amusement was exactly what Mother would have preferred we not partake of.

An example: On a windy day, a well-dressed but overweight woman might pass down the sidewalk, and Dad would say, "I'm very fancy and high society but I'm luckiest of all to have a big bottom in this stiff wind."

That would be enough to throw my sister and me into convulsions. Then a thin man might come along, and Dad would say, "I'm lucky in this wind to be a bean-pole."

And off we'd go again in a gale of laughter. It clearly didn't take much to amuse us waiting on some busy city street for Mom to get done whatever she had to get done in the real world. But when she did come towards the car with a package or other, it gave Dad the best opportunity yet to do his thing: "Here I am in a big hurry to get back to the car. And Tom, I hope, has the kids all settled down or napping." And that would crack us up with a vengeance. But before Dad could open the door to let Mom in, my sister and I would put on our poker faces, and Dad would become a serious gentleman. Once in the car, quiet now as a dam holding back water, Mom would glance around at us in the backseat and then directly at Tom, who was starting the car. "What?!" she'd say, and then the dam would break and everyone, except poor Mom, was laughing.

We could laugh at my mother that way because we loved her, and we could laugh at the passers-by because, in the first instance, they didn't know we were laughing at them, and, in the second instance, because we didn't know who they were and, frankly, we didn't love them.

24 THE CASE OF THE SNARED DRUMMERS

HAPPINESS, LIKE A winter wren singing in an old growth forest, was when I maneuvered Dad into his favorite chair for evening story telling. (Story yelling?) After my repeated tugging on his pants legs, he'd hoist me into the air and place me on his knee. Whatever conversation was in progress between him and my mother scattered like startled crows before the oncoming story bus.

It wasn't really widely different stories that he told. The tales were episodic, adventure-driven narratives that suddenly could degenerate into mayhem. These were not stories of any particular moral instruction nor were they revered classics from Dad's home in Ireland, though he might have told that kind of thing to my sister. ("Tell me again, Father, the tale of 'Cuchulain's Wooing.'")

These were also not stories about the Founding Fathers of our great nation who all wore powdered wigs like classical composers but had servants who played better piano; nor were they tales of early settlement days of Montesano, when only churches and one saloon existed, and everyone who lived in Montesano came from back east with pioneer women dressed in skirts with attached aprons.

These were not sports stories either as you might suspect from my passion for the "long ball," the "hook shot," and the "Hail Mary," nor fictions of literary value.

Actually, I don't know what these stories were. "Strange" comes to mind (but "terribly absorbing"). But let my Dad tell one story to you rather than me tell you about him telling it to me. Let us go to the warm fire-lit living room of my old Montesano home, where Dad has just retrieved from the bookshelf of

125

his mind the bound-in-leather "Case of the Snared Drummers":

I was burning utility bills at my desk in my clinic on Main Street, when my secretary, the efficient and slim, Miss Waters . . .

"Tom," my mother warns from across the living room where she is sewing buttons on my sister's coat. My sister, by the way, is on the floor cutting out furniture pictures from a Sears and Roebuck catalog and pasting them in a cardboard box she has convinced herself is her future dream house. Only when I was a little bored and greatly weakened in mental faculties would I, with her, participate in this cut-and-paste diversion. Our discovery of the technology for making paste from ordinary flour encouraged us in this direction.

"Sorry, Hon," my father replies, with a wink to me.

My plump secretary, Mrs. Waters, informed me that I had an international call. Not much had been happening since my last case "The Hunt for Miss October."

"Tom."

I picked up the receiver and on a line thumping with background noise made out the bad English of my old African friend, Dr. Wambuui.

"I remember him," I note.

"That's right, son. He featured in our "Case of the Missing Thumb Harp."

"Dr. O'Connor, is that you?"

"Yes, Dr. Wambuui, it is Dr. O'Connor in Montesano."

"Dr. O'Connor, thank the River Gods I've reached you. We need your help. Zaibu, our village, is threatened again by the giant snake Menabi. Can you help us? Is it possible you could come to Africa and get this thing out of our hair?

"Where are you calling from, Doctor?"

"Sir, where do you think I'm calling from?"

"May I have twenty questions?"

"Dr. O'Connor, we have no time for games. We're losing our villagers! I'm calling from Zaibu, of course."

"I thought as much, but tell me Doctor, indulge me just a little: What is that noise in the background?"

126

"It's the village drums. Their rhythmic patterns in some hypnotic way keep Menabi at bay."

"That's charming, Doctor. But has Menabi eaten anyone yet," I asked.

"Several children are missing. Though they might be just playing hooky."

"Anyone else? You must understand, Dr. Wambuui, I must be absolutely thorough, though at this point I'm not altogether sure why."

"Menabi may have eaten others, Dr. O'Connor, but we won't know until we can do an autopsy, assuming we, you can acquire a cutting torch."

"What's an autopsy, Dad?"

"That's when you examine a body after a person dies," Father says cheerfully.

"Why would anyone want to do that?"

"Well, just as Dr. Wambuui said, to find out who is inside the stomach of Menabi. In effect, it's a kind of census taking."

"Oh."

"Listen, Dr. Wambuui. I'll come immediately. I'm also going to bring my son, Mike. He's been with me on similar cases and proved very helpful; plus it's kept him out of trouble."

"Wonderful, Dr. O'Connor. The village is poor but we'll manage to pay you something. Would you, for instance, accept from us a second wife?"

I look across the room at Mother, but she is bent over her sewing, a thread between her teeth and a thimble on her finger.

"I'll pass on that, Dr. Wambuui, you don't have to pay us. You should know this from my reputation, my past cases."

"Actually, Doctor, it is why the village council insisted I contact you first."

"Perfectly reasonable, Dr. Wambuui, but let me ask, when was it Zaibu got telephones?"

About here, Dad shifts me to his other knee and we land on the African Continent in Zaibu.

When I and my son attained the torch-lit village, with its well-crafted circle of mud huts, Dr. Wambuui and his assistants, fully dressed, came out of the village clinic waving Montesano Bulldog pennants to greet us. "You can put those aside," I said, beaming with Bulldog pride.

According to the good doctor, Menabi had entered the village briefly the night before (the snake!) and had dined on the two village drummers who, inopportunely, had taken a set-break to sign autographs for Zaibu groupies. The village was now without proper drum defense.

"We need to go after Menabi without delay, while he's still digesting the drummers,"

I said.

"How will you subdue him? Dr. O'Connor?"

"In my pack, I have a tranquilizer gun from a former case called, 'The Imposter Santa Claus at the Saturday Matinee.'"

"What was that about, Doctor O'Connor?"

"I'm sorry, but the information is declassified."

"Oh."

"Anyway, once I've sedated Menabi, I'll administer an extract of my wife's cooking—the Spam recipe should do it—and . . . my mother's head rises . . . which will curb his appetite for years to come.

My mother shakes her head from side to side, but goes on sewing.

Oh, and my son has a magic flute."

"Haydn?"

"No. Would you like twenty questions, Dr. Wambuui?"

"You've got me there, Doctor O'Connor. Brahms?"

"Anyway, after we've got Menabi in tow, you can install him in the schoolyard as a long slide, or kink him up for a jungle gym. No pun intended."

128

"Wonderful, Doctor O'Connor. Would you also like some Zaibu warriors to accompany you? We can clothe them, and they know the jungle habitat like they know the tattoos on the back of their hands, since, of course, they live here."

"I know they do, Dr. Wambuui, but this mission isn't a training one. My son and I have a better chance alone. It would take too long to introduce and subsequently develop more fictional characters. But hey, thanks, Doc. And tell your warriors, maybe next time. I know their hearts are in the right place."

My son and I set out immediately, pushing through the thick jungle underbrush, which was much easier to do than get through second-growth timber along the Wynooche River looking for cranberry bogs around Thanksgiving.

By early afternoon, we came to a broad yellow tributary of the Zambizi River, and, just as we reached it, a herd of zebras on the opposite shore scared up, thundered, and clicked away on the adjacent plain looking just like an edition of the *Montesano Vidette* being printed once a week.

A herd of giraffes also fled, their long necks resembling a schoolyard of jump ropes swinging in the clouds. In the stream itself, which we had to cross because it was there, a dozen crocodiles smiled at us like a row of used cars with their hoods open on Honest Al's used-car lot on First Street. I told my son, Mike, Mike O'Connor of 102 North Sylvia Street, Montesano, Washington, that we'd have to cross the stream on the heads of the crocodiles.

"Think of it as hopscotch," I told him. "Hazardous Hopscotch" or a crock hop.

Son Mike, did not flinch, waver, or vacillate, and jumped on the head of the first old croc (who later complained, "Hey, I wasn't ready!").

Mike went on across the river never missing a beat, nor the head of a crocodile, which all resembled nubby manhole covers. I followed the brave example of my son, but just as I prepared to leap to the last manhole cover, it turned into a gaping, vicious used car.

"He's not at his desk right now!!!! He's not at his desk right now!!!!" my son yelled from the shore.

The cry, so surprised the used-car crocodile that he immediately turned into a compliant manhole cover again. I landed on the crock's pebbled head instead of on his luncheon menu, and then jumped the last distance to shore.

"Good work, Son," I said.

"Thanks, Father."

"Where did you learn that call?"

"From your secretary, plump Mrs. Waters."

My son and I proceeded across the grass-savannah plain. A lion or lioness lay in the shade of a twisted Morocco tree, but preoccupied with digesting a he or she zebra, he or she did not see Mike or me. But Mike and I saw him or her, and what we saw looked like pages of the *Montesano Vidette* dripping from his or her jaws.

We finally re-entered the jungle which I would estimate was thirty drum beats from the village of Zaibu. I told my son there were signs now that Menabi was in the neighborhood, if you could call this rank forest a neighborhood.

"What were the signs, Dad?

"Well, Son, one said, *Welcome, home of Menabi, make yourself comfortable under any picnic tree.* A second said, *Good luck, ha, ha!"*

It grew darker and darker as we penetrated farther and farther, deeper and deeper darker and farther, deeper darker farther, darker, deeper and farther . . .

"Tom."

. . . into the jungle. Then I heard something astir in the big ocea tree before us. I put my hand on my son's shoulder he puts his hand on my shoulder to stop his progress and whispered, he whispers in my ear "I think it's Menabi."

My son instinctively went to my backpack and expertly removed the tranquilizer gun still in its monkey-tail case without disturbing the peanut butter sandwiches or the Oreo cookies. He handed it to me and then we hunkered down and waited in the living lower world of that snake-eat-snake, snake-eat-anything-available jungle. As I removed the gun from its case, I realized it was my left-handed putter.

"Mike," I whispered. "Look at this."

"Father, do you think this is the time to work on your putting?"

"No, of course not. Mrs. Waters packed my putter by mistake."

"Fear not, Father. We still have my magic flute."

From time to time, we could hear far up in the great ocea tree a big snake stomach digesting drummers. It sounded more like a muffled band warming up than a band in full swing. My son noted that it sounded more like a band warming down than up. It was at moments like this, in cases like this on such missions as this that I felt pride in my son's droll sense of humor. "You're very Irish," son, I said.

"Thanks, Father." Mike said with respectful bewilderment.

About this time in the story I'm getting on edge about the near presence of Old Menabi (who I knew from many former stories), but I am also nervous because I know, both loving and fearing it as I did, the moment we sighted him, Dad would feign a cry of alarm, lift me from his lap, and throw me totally freaked-out into the air.

My son and I waited so long several new trees sprouted from the fertile humus of the jungle floor. The enzymatic ruminative drumming, like a machine tumbling agates to a polish, was getting faint, and we knew that if we didn't act soon, the drummers would be playing harps in Zaibu heaven rather than percussion in Zaibu village.

Menabi was lolling unseen in the top of the ocea tree, feeling expansive and digging the muted rhythms now closer to his tail than to the built-in headset of his lobe-less ears. The world is good,

Menabi was thinking, basking in the sunlight of the upper canopy. "If I had a good South African cigar right now, the world would be perfect."

But bliss eluded Menabi, and he began to feel a craving for dessert—perhaps a monkey or a baby warthog. He gazed down through the ocea branches and leaves to the market place of the jungle floor, and, lo and behold, spotted a furry old anteater who had just passed us with his long snout and tiny eyes glued to the forest floor. The anteater looked a lot like an usher at a movie house searching with a flashlight for a patron's lost wallet.

The anteater was just the bait we needed to get Menabi out of the tree. It was serendipitous.

"Seren what?" I ask.

"It was fortunate, but unplanned."

The anteater, the pre-occupied scholar of the animal kingdom, nosed around right under the ocea tree having espied, I presume, a worker ant heading home dragging eye parts of a dead fly for supper.

Though my son and I had only sensed Menabi's presence in the ocea tree, we now felt with certainty at any moment Menabi, all one hundred revolting feet of evil that he was, was about to drop whooosh and kaplunk from the tree, like a fanged Goodyear blimp,

"A fanged Goodyear blimp?" I say.

"Something like that."

The anteater, the jungle scholar, was unaware of the steely-cold eyes of Menabi, and old Menabi, like a long train with slippers on began to depart the railway station, slithering slowly, slowly across the upper outspread branches of the ocea tree. It took him forever to leave the station.

It is coming, now, I know. The big moment is coming!

Slowly, slowly Menabi moved into position to give the bookish anteater a big surprise. But suddenly something he saw forestalled his horrid plunge. Nearby the anteater was a young boy, who looked even more delicious and much less hairy than the the scholar of the jungle. He had not yet seen me, however, his old nemesis, Dr. O'Connor; which was fortunate because it gave me time to pray for my son.

Slowly, slowly Menabi moved across the tree crowns, positioning himself for an attack on Mike ("Our Father who art in Heaven . . ."). Slowly, slowly he glistered along a huge branch of the ocea tree resembling a hormonal-hydroponic cucumber or, if you prefer, a huge strand of spaghetti in search of a meatball.

Circling above his prey, as Menabi was genetically programed to do, the huge snake passed from the ocea tree, known for its sweet fruit and the strength to support abnormally large serpents; to the heliocapacius tree, reputed to have salutary properties for curing ataxia, dementia, and vomiting; to the doxianna tree, first scientifically identified by Dr. Livingstone and now known for the property of its leaves, namely, despite their rainbow colors, no property of any value at all, except aesthetic, which is pretty much the same thing; to the Timbuktu willow, which birds loved above all others and built small villages each year in their branches and even temples and libraries; to the shingles-fermentia-galoshes tree, whose flowers have the fragrance of Paris and the Elwha River, and whose bark is resistant to mud and spitting.

Finally, Menabi was in position to drop in on my son, but Mike, senses keen as a rabbit, had been watching Menabi ever since his 100-foot fire hose had passed over the crown of the heliocapacious tree, whose salutary properties cure ataxia, dementia and vomiting, though not all in the same day; and as I rose and shook myself from prayer and regained my putter, Mike pulled from his pocket his magic flute and began to toot.

I must confess, I had wanted Mike to take saxophone lessons so someday he could play in a big band in college and pay his own tuition, room and board, but at this moment, I was grateful he was conversant on the small one-hole flute an ex-sawyer-turned-witch-doctor in the hills south of Montesano had made for him from cascara wood in an exchange for boxing trading cards.

The notes of the flute floated like soap and water bubbles from a plastic pipe sweetly into the dense upper reaches of the jungle. And then: miracle of miracles! Menabi, like a big soap bubble himself burst in a rainbow spray of hideous scales, and vanished! A hundred feet of twilight suddenly was restored above us. A few first jungle stars appeared like birthday candles on a space cake.

"You did it, Son; Menabi is gone."

"Yes, father, but the magic flute has only temporarily de-materialized Menabi. I needed to give Elmer, the ex-sawyer with the missing thumb and now resident witch doctor, a Joe Lewis card, which is rare, in order to get the two-hole flute for Permanent Dissolution of Evil Entities (PDEE). In fact, Father, I should apologize to you for so hastily defending myself, not waiting for you to use the left-handed putter, though surely old Menabi was after my young person for dessert."

"Nonsense, son, what was I doing all this time? Why I was praying there in the leaf-mold for another son just in case the magic flute was a dud. In other words, I was thinking only of myself."

"No, Father, your interpretation is inaccurate. You were thinking, of our family name. Nothing could be nobler than that."

"Well, if you put it that way. But too bad about the Joe Lewis card."

My son and I had been in the jungle too long; our minds were tangled with vines of feeling, branches of thought, roots of sensations, mosses of confusion. We were thinking of never taking a bath again.

"Let's get back to the village, it will be dark soon," I said. "I need to turn off my brain."

"Good idea, Father."

"You mean, good idea to turn my brain off or to return to the village?"

"The village, but of course, Father."

Meanwhile, not far from this scene, the Evil One, the Snake that Can't Be Tread On, the Great Recycler of Jungle Wild Life, The High Priest of Low Living, Menabi, was slowly re-materializing. It was fortunate for Menabi that he re-materialized without any part of his body being misarranged. Had Menabi been a 500-piece jig-saw puzzle, only his head would have been able to be put together properly, so much of the rest of him looked the same.

Menabi then spoke to himself these words: "For crying out loud, wouldn't you know it, just when I'm on a good run, who shows up with a putter and a magic flute? None other than Dr. O'Connor of Montesano and that second grader, Mike. Nertz! Double nertz!!"

At the mention of the Doctor's surname, and from far within the inner tunnel of Menabi's digestive tract, which pretty much was all Menabi was, a digestive tract, came the faint sound of revived drumming, beating softly with new hope.

"I was just moments away from adding the kid as a flautist to my garage band," continued Menabi. "I admit, the bookings are short-lived, however. HA HA HA. The bookings are short-lived. Oh, Menabi, you are a real something! HA HA HA.

"But think not I re-materialize here on this savannah plain for idle jesting, or for that matter gestation or digestion only. No, hardly, for I have a plan that fits the serpent nature of my mind to the serpent nature of my body and the serpent nature of these truly serpent times, as these writhing sentences I utter between my outsized fangs attest.

"But hark thee. Do I hear the hapless hunters approaching now the river of this vast savannah plain? Let me get my hundred feet of snake offstage so I may freely soon again—spared of the O'Connors—patronize my favorite smorgasbord, the village of Zaibu."

Quite a bit later when Menabi had finally managed to get all of himself off stage and several more trees had sprouted from the jungle floor, I and my son, approached the river. I had been worrying how we might cross it at night, since it would be impossible to make perfect landings on the heads of the crocodiles. Night was usually dark in these parts and hard to see in.

"How will we cross the river, Father?"

"I've been thinking about that, Son. I don't suppose that magic flute of yours could de-materialize it for a while."

"No, Father. It has no such powers."

"I wonder if the crocs are sleeping; I wonder if the piranha are swimming about looking for fast food; I wonder if you were to wade out a ways, son, and test the waters for us, just a little."

"I could, Father, but what if the crocodiles or the piranha are there?"

"Good point, son. We really need a lifeline for you. If they attacked I'd at least be able to bring part of you back to Montesano with me."

Tom O'Connor! That's just too much. It's time Mike went to bed! I'm not sure which one of you is the child.

I then suggested to my son that we speed up the adventure. "Let's speed up the adventure and explore the riverbanks. Perhaps we can find a ferryman, a discarded raft, or perhaps a place where the sandbars narrow the waterway."

It was dark and African along the riverbank. A thousand million stars shone like New York City. In fact, we could see the light pollution of that city in the west like a murky errant branch of the Milky Way.

The cry of an eagledooriana suddenly pierced the serenity. It sent chills down my spine, and I presume, up Mike's or vice versa or versa vice. The chills were justified. The eagledooriana was a car owner's or butterfly collector's nightmare, weighing 200 pounds with a wingspan of thirty feet. Its droppings were capable of reaching the center of the earth, unless obstructed by elephants, tribesmen, or bird watchers. The only predator of the eagledooriana was Menabi.

Just then, in a great fanning of wings, the eagledooriana flew up from the bent-to-near-breaking tree where it had perched, and flapped into the night sky. Something had startled it. We looked but could only see, wonder of wonders, there! spanning a wide reach of the river, a great fallen tree, a lot like the ones over the Queets River in Washington, but this one was de-limbed and looked to afford easy crossing.

"Look, Son. A log bridge."

"Yes, Father. But how did we miss seeing it this afternoon?"

When we gained the bridge I went first followed closely by Mike. The log was wide enough that passage initially went well, but a slippery quality of the log's surface where the bark had evidently been peeled was hazardous.

"Be careful, Son, this log is slippery as an eel."

As we gingerly crossed, we were surprised to hear faint sounds from the village.

"Can you hear the drums, Mike? They must have found some replacements for the two drummers Menabi ate."

"But I would have thought, Father, we are too far from the village.

Halfway across the bridge,

I know it is finally going to come this time. I brace myself. I'm as ready as I can be.

I called time out, took out my pipe and lit it while waiting for my son to catch up.

"Oh, you're right behind me," I said, as Mike almost bumped me into the river.

"Africa," I said. "There is nothing like this land for enjoying a good smoke."

A harmless yakoo bird screeched from the sandy shore. It sounded like a robin with its heart ripped out.

"Tom, that's it. Mike, off to bed with you. "

"Okay, okay, Shirley, the story's almost over."

"A robin with its heart torn out," Mom mutters to herself, shaking her head and leaving the room.

"So where was I?"

"Pipe smoking on the bridge."

"Ah, Africa. What a mood it gives a man of the outdoors," I said to my son. "Someday, this will all be yours."

"We'd better push on Father, we still have miles to go before we sleep," said Mike.

"Yes, of course," I said, knocking out the ash from my pipe on the heel of my boot.

I began again crossing to the other shore. Suddenly, "Yikes," I almost slipped off the bridge.

"Father." shouted my son.

"I'm all right, but this bridge is even more slippery than an eel."

We fearlessly continued crossing, walking steadily for ten minutes, then ten minutes more; we kept walking just as if we were on a treadmill.

"Father," said Mike. "Have you noticed we've been walking across the bridge for a very long time, that we are, in fact, across the river yet the bridge continues ahead of us through the forest, that the bridge in fact is MOVING UNDER US?!"

"Yiiiiiiiiiiiiiiiiiiiiiiiiiiiiiiiiiiiiiiiiiiiiiiikes!!!!!!!!!!"

Dad, emitting a wild and prolonged YIKES, lifts me from his lap and tosses me high in the air, then catches me in his arms.

Menabi faced us with open jaws as wide as the doors of an airplane hanger; his eyes were great globes of cold fire burning like twin movie projectors. Just as he got all of the coordinates in his head straightened out and readied to devour us, Mike, drew out his magic flute and, without blowing a single note, hurled it like a rock deep into the mouth of the monster. Menabi, taken aback, paused just long enough for me to abruptly query my son, "Are you crazy? We were counting on the powers of the flute."

"I don't have much time to explain, Father, but I fear once again I may have overstepped my filial boundaries."

"Speak English, my son. It is why we send you to public school."

Fortunately, Menabi, taken by surprise, needed a few seconds to burp the magic flute into his deeper recesses.

"My intention was to send the magic flute to the captured drummers. If they play a tune on it, it will de-materialize Menabi but leave them whole."

Burp over, Menabi reared up one more time and prepared to strike, but just as his terrible snake breath fogged up our eyes and made us recall the pulp mills of Washington (particularly Tacoma and Everett); we could hear notes of the flute floating up the long tunnel like a donkey caravan to the open air.

"Drat!" said Menabi. "I'm de-materialized again. But before I go, O'Connor, tell that stupid Dr. Wambuui, 'The Magic Flute,' it's Mozart!" And then he vanished, grudgingly.

Two very exhausted village warriors (they were all drummed out) now lay before us on the jungle grass. "Hello boys," I greeted them. "Remember, to rest is not to conquer."

"We knew it was you, Doctor O'Connor. We never gave up hope."

"Have you seen any hooky players around here or in there where you were possibly with them lately?"

"No, Sir. I think the boys went swimming at Lake Victoria."

"Well, then," I said. "All's well that end's well."

"Yes, Sir. Doctor O'Connor, Sir." And the drummer weakly waved a badly slimed and tattered Montesano Bulldog-welcome-to-Zaibu pennant.

Within an hour we had reached the village. It was bedtime there, everyone snug and terrified in their well-crafted clay beds; but the villagers poured from their huts as soon as word went out that I, my son, and the two drummers had safely returned.

Dr. Wambuui was profuse in his thanks on behalf of the whole village. There was much square dancing and limbo-ing, but since it was Friday and in deference to our Christian ways, no meat was served at the feast, and the cannibal events were postponed until the following week.

I informed the drummers that they could keep the magic flute for subsequent encounters with Menabi but that they must be absolutely vigilant in using the technology for good and never for evil.

"I understand, Doctor," said one of the drummers, with a funny smile.

"Where's the other drummer?" I asked.

The festivities went on into the late hours, and at one point, just before everyone went off to bed again, Dr. Wambuui introduced his beautiful young daughter to my son and me. "Mike, this is my daughter, Congo-Funicello. Congo, this is Mike."

Congo was wearing Mickey Mouse ears, she being president of the Zaibu Mickey Mouse Club, and a number of temporary tattoos.

Congo came forward gracefully and stood before Mike. "For your brave acts on behalf of my father and Zaibu, I wish to present to you this magic potion from the last uficadora tree spared from slash and burn."

"I'm hardly worthy of it," said my son. "What does the potion do."

"You will find that out in the next installment of Doctor O'Connor, in "The Case of Something Else Missing.""

And with that, Congo planted a kiss with her lip ring on the cheek of my son, who blushed brighter than the one stoplight in Montesano, and then everyone all over Africa said, "Good night, Dr. O'Connor, good-night, Mike."

And, no longer fearing Menabi, Dr. Wambuui, on our sleeping

porch at the clinic, turned out the torches, and muttered, "Rimsky-Korsakov?"

"No."

"Bach?"

"Warmer, Dr. Wambuui, warmer."

25 DAREDEVILS

AT THE BEST time of the year (O sun-filled August), Grays Harbor held its county fair. Once they had a daredevils' grandstand show after the harness races. It was very exciting and better than the trotters, and it spawned a daring week of deviltry in my backyard.

Part of the show was stockcars jumping from ramps over other stockcars to other ramps. Usually the driver made it, and after coming safely down the off-ramp, he'd drive up the track, turn around sharply in a plume of dust, barrel back in front of the grandstand, and slam on his brakes. The car door would fly open and out would jump the grinning daredevil to take a bow. Our hands got raw from clapping.

One time, a car got a blown tire and crashed into the down-ramp, crumpling the front fenders of the car; but the driver climbed out unscathed and still took a bow. We clapped even harder for him.

"The roll-bar saved him," a spectator explained.

Towards the end of the show, a crew in jump suits removed the ramps and erected a wooden wall. Someone squiggled a can of gasoline on it and lighted it. A car came down the track and straight into and through the burning wall. Part of the wall clung to the car as it passed through, so the driver accelerated to over a hundred miles per hour, which blew the flames out. Then he drove back in front of the grandstand, jumped out, and took a bow.

"That took grit," said a cigar-smoking stranger in front of me. But that wasn't the end. The best was yet to come. A man, assisted by a tall woman in a bathing suit, stuffed himself—with some assistance from the tall woman—into a coffin filled with dynamite. The announcer said no one had ever done this trick with so much dynamite before. I was surprised anyone had ever done the trick with any dynamite before. The announcer added that in order to protect the spectators a shield would be put up between us and the coffin. The crew of men in jump suits then raced out and fitted together a shield that was to protect the spectators and that blocked our view of the coffin. Then the crew and tall woman in a bathing suit hurried up the track out of range and the coffin blew up.

It took a few moments for the smoke to clear, but when it did, there was the daredevil! You could tell he'd been blown up because his clothing was burned and tattered, and his face was black as coal. He held his arms aloft in triumph and then made a series of bows, and everyone in the grandstand stood up and clapped themselves silly.

Riding home on my side of the backseat from the Elma fairgrounds, I fell asleep and dreamed of shiny, speeding, crashing cars, and a burning wall. That weekend I and the Rachet boys from up the alley and Leroy Simmons from down the street got right to work building jump ramps for our bicycles. The first ramps were low, and we found we could fly from one to the other quite effortlessly. We built higher ramps and higher ramps until we could no longer ride fast enough to carry us to the off-or down-ramp, as we flew into space willy-nilly and smacked into the ground, crashing in some reckless, albeit usually fun-to-watch, improvised manner. Leroy Simmons, however, broke his thumb when the handlebars of his bike came off in mid-air and he crashed. He lay on the ground howling so loud we feared someone's mother would come. We huddled around him and finally got him to calm down. Then we sent him home to get his thumb fixed, but not before we had to give him a round of applause and to instruct him not to tell his mother that it had happened doing one of our daredevil stunts. We also made him promise to send his younger brother, Freddie, as a replacement.

Up to this point, my parents and certain weekend guests of my parents had randomly observed us from the kitchen at the back of our house. Up to this point, also, my parents had only voiced mild concern that we might be tearing up the lawn and perhaps being too rough on our bicycles. We were doing both. Our bicycles, for instance, were starting to resemble incomplete Kooties, from the game of that name. Dad's lawn was looking increasing like a high school football field after the last game of the season. What is more, after two days of ramp-jumping, we boys agreed that riding girls' bikes would have made a lot more sense, have been a lot safer and more comfortable, but we didn't have any girl bikes, and we were sure no girl was going to lend us theirs for our demolition-like stunts.

Aside from Leroy's broken thumb and our sore scrotums, we daredevils hadn't sustained any injuries. The broken thumb was just the result of a freak mechanical or structural failure. Heck, in football some kid was always losing teeth, spraining ankles, or getting nose bleeds.

Probably the highlight of our show, the most artful part, was when we set up all the wooden ramps we had made and tried synchronized jumps. That meant at least three riders jumping simultaneously and then turning around and changing ramps with each other, weaving dangerously close in the transitions. Ultimately we had a lot of crashes and a lot of fun.

Not surprisingly, though, someone got the idea to blow one of us up like the man in the coffin at the fairgrounds. There was initial interest. It would be a proper way to conclude our daredevil folies. Everyone gathered around to consider it. We glanced about the yard but to my relief (I was a moron not a fool) no one could see anything resembling a coffin and no one had a clue where we could latch onto dynamite. But we did have wood for making a burning wall, and we knew where we could get gasoline and matches. The real question before us, however, was: who, once we erected the burning wall, would be brave enough to ride through it; who, in other words, had the *grit?*

The older Ratchet boy, Terry, siphoned gas from his father's old Nash Rambler that had been retired to the backyard under an old pitchy cherry tree. We reminded Terry not to linger at the gas tank, sniffing or swallowing the gas, because we knew he liked getting dizzy. Johnny, the younger Rachet, helped me tear some of the boards off our stalled addition to the Fort. We quickly constructed a pre-fabricated, rather flimsy wall in the yard, and Jerry came along with a jug of siphoned gasoline and stolen wooden matches from the Ratchet's kitchen.

We were fascinated with the burning wall stunt; our preparations had sharpened our senses to the danger of it. This stunt would be our grand finale. It had to be because our wagons, soapbox cars, skates, and bikes were mostly all busted from our daredeviltry. My beloved Columbia Racer, for instance, was held together now by wire and rope, and looked a lot like the clown's bike in Montesano's Tree-farm Parade.

So on the last day of our performances, we hammered up the burning wall and fixed it in place using guy ropes as when securing a tent. The wind waved it a little, but it held. Terry said he'd pour the gas on it and light it. That would be his role, he made clear, "so choose someone else to ride." That left Little Johnny, myself, and Leroy's replacement as candidates. Leroy's replacement, Freddie, was frankly too young, and I didn't want any part of it either, being frankly older. I had been tempted to talk the Little Replacement into it, but the better angel of my nature overruled the other angels.

So Little Johnny and I flipped a coin and I lost.

"How about two out of three," I said.

I lost again.

"Okay, I get to do it," I said. I picked up my bicycle and putting a big phony smile on my face, said to Johnny, "This will make me King of the Daredevils."

"It will?" said Little Johnny.

"Oh, most certainly it will. Move aside there, I need to get set," I said, pushing the front wheel of my bike over his foot. "The King of the Daredevils is coming."

"If I do the stunt, can I be King of the Daredevils?"

"Well, I'm not sure, Johnny."

"Why not? I've done just about all the stunts you've done."

"Hey, are you guys ready," yelled Terry. "I'm not going to hold this gasoline can all day."

"I'll tell you what. If I let you do the stunt and you get to be King of the Daredevils, will you let me at least lend you my football helmet as an honor to me and to protect you?"

"I can't see anything if I wear a helmet. But I'll ride your bike."

"Fair enough," I said. "It's my honor."

I dismounted and gave him my woebegone bicycle—fender-less, frame-bent—and he walked it over to the starting ramp. The course was laid out so Little Johnny would start under the pear tree, go up and over the low ramp, up and over a second higher ramp, then straight through the burning wall. We had placed a pail of water by the wall to use in case Little Johnny caught on fire.

"Can I light it now?" yelled Terry.

"Hold your fire a second," I yelled back. "Johnny's getting ready."

I held out my crash football helmet to Johnny, but he swept it aside like Ceasar turning down a chance to be emperor.

"Are you ready?" I asked.

"Tell Terry to light the wall."

"Light the wall," I yelled.

Terry flung the gas from his plastic jug onto the wall, but couldn't get a match struck for several moments as vapors built up. Then he did, and blew himself up. The wall was burning, and at the sound of the explosion, Johnny took off over the low ramp and headed full steam up the higher one.

But as he neared the burning wall, he saw his brother lying flat on his back on the ground in wreaths of flame, and at the last moment swerved away from the wall of fire, and rode into the high hedge at the end of my yard. I rushed to where Terry was lying dazed, picked up the pail of water, and doused him. Sputtering, he struggled to his feet, and with his blackened face, torn shirt, and no eyebrows, he looked like the daredevil at the county fair who blew himself up in a coffin.

"Are you okay," I asked.

He nodded. Then Little Johnny climbed out of the hedge, apparently unscathed, and assisted his brother in walking home up the alley. The Little Replacement kid and I fetched more water and put out the flames on what was left of the wall, now mostly smoke and charred sticks.

"Wow," said the Little Replacement kid, "That was something."

"It went fairly well, didn't it?"

"I'll say. And Terry had the best trick yet. Wow."

"Little Johnny rode bravely also," I noted.

"And he's King of the Daredevils now, isn't he?"

"Yes, I guess he is," I conceded.

"Wow," said the Little Replacement kid. "Wow."

"Freddy, would you like to be a daredevil when you grow up?"

"No."

26 DIGGING TO CHINA

I.

ONE AFTERNOON IN August, Terry and Johnny Rachet, and I were resting on the grass in my backyard in the shade of our old plum tree. With our mitts and bats, we were waiting for Leroy Simmons and Gary Short to arrive and start a baseball game. And while we waited, we began talking about geography. What got us going in that direction was just the week before the three of us and two other members of our Cub Scout den had put on a skit at the library, organized by our den mother, my mom. The different Cub Scout dens in town all participated, and the theme of each den's skit was a foreign country, one different from America, in other words.

Our den's choice of country was China. So we, with big help from the carpentry skills of Terry Ratchet and Nolan Peterson, built a palanquin from a busted wagon, which four kids could carry and one kid could ride in. Nolan, by the way, was an adult who knew my Dad from work. He lived in a town called Raymond, thirty or so miles away on the other side of the Chehalis River. About the only time I ever rode across the long Chehalis Bridge in South Monte was when our family drove to Raymond to visit Nolan and his family. Nolan had a pretty dark-complexioned wife and a daughter younger than I and also pretty. The three of them appeared in our home movies quite a lot; they were very photogenic.

But then something went wrong. Nolan would frequently come to Montesano and stay with us. It was usually during the weekdays and my father would be on the road doing Department of Agriculture work. Nolan would talk with my mother in the kitchen (they drank lots of coffee), and it was apparent to both my sister and me that Nolan was miserable. His wife didn't love him anymore, is what it was about, my mother finally told us.

Whenever Nolan came, he'd have long talks with my mom and then sleep on the couch in the living room. I guessed while he was trying to hold his marriage together and avoid being served divorce papers, he needed to clear out of his house so he could think, and to talk to someone who wasn't the problem.

More than once, he offered to help me with a Cub Scout project. He made—with some help from me—a beautiful birdhouse, for example. He was a kind man and I got to like his visiting us, and he seemed to like my putting him to work.

But the marriage dispute went to the courthouse. And whoever was running things on the top marble floor, gave his dark pretty wife a divorce. I don't know what they gave Nolan, but it wasn't much. My dad helped him transfer to another town out of state and I never saw him again. But he and Terry Rachet did a really great job on that palanquin.

To decide who would carry it and who would ride, our den drew straws, and thanks to the luck of the Irish, I got to ride. But I also—at some point in the skit—had to step out of the palanquin and read, or talk about, China to the audience for educational purposes. It was the fare for the ride, I figured.

At the international event that evening, right off our den got things messed up. We went on stage too early, before the Mexico den had finished. My den brothers and our palanquin ran right over a kid in a big sombrero who was simulating a siesta on a Mexican rug. My mother in the first row stood up and waved us frantically back to the wings. "Not yet," she whispered fiercely. "Not yet."

I think she also whispered, "For god's sakes, children!"

We managed to get turned around but ran smack into some of the other kids dressed as Mexicans who were trying to drag their dazed siesta amigo to the wings. I may have failed to mention that the five of us representing China had nylon stockings over our heads so our eyes would pull up to look like Chinamen's. I think our look contributed to some of the turmoil that was now breaking out on the stage. The kids representing Mexico were shouting and running back and forth across the stage. Their big cactus, made of papier-mache and thin plywood and occupying center stage, got knocked over in one swipe by our palanquin. The nylon stockings were making it impossible for my carriers to see where they were going. We also looked, I think, like bank robbers.

With the Mexico skit now in disarray and, by default, over, my carriers finally set the palanquin down, and taking a deep breath, I officiously stepped out of the car and over the dismembered cactus. I waited until the hall quieted—there were moms rushing to check on their Mexico charges back stage—and then delivered my talk, slash, reading.

I spoke loftily of China's population (there's more of them than us); of chopsticks (where the piano piece of that name comes from); of fireworks (they invented them for our Fourth of July); of printing (they didn't get it quite right and have to read their books back to front); of the Great Wall (they started with the idea to keep their dogs in, but ended with the idea to keep other dogs out); and of rice (they have never heard of the potato or white bread and always are hungry soon after meals). As you can see, I was making the subject interesting for the audience.

And I was getting good laughs and only wished I'd prepared more material. Not everyone understood what I was saying. At that age, I still had a detectable speech impediment, so I needed to go slow. My speech problem, ironically, worked more for me that evening than against me, however. I had great difficulty pronouncing the consonant 'r.' The word "railroad" for instance, I pronounced lail-load, while a word like "raillery," I wouldn't have been able to pro-nounce at all.

But on stage that evening when I said "lice" for rice and "lailload" for railroad, why a lot of folks thought I was speaking Chinese, or at least imitating it pretty well. But what that nylon stocking con-tributed to my overall stage effect is difficult to measure.

Though our den probably set relations with China and our local library staff back at least a dynasty (I'm sure Mexican and Chinese relations henceforward also suffered), I must say I felt the evening overall was a triumph. In our magnanimity, our den donated the palanquin to the library. Mrs. Kendel, head librarian, appeared over-whelmed by the gesture, but, curiously, we never saw the painted palanquin again.

That night I had my recurring Zorro dream. He rode up to the farm where I was gathering eggs, but unlike the usual dream, where I give him a dozen brown ones, I didn't have any eggs to give him, white, brown, or green. Another twist in the dream was that I was with my den brothers, rather than by myself, and we were all wear-ing nylon stockings over our heads.

"What are you doing here," said Zorro from the back of his horse. He drew out his sword and added, "Who are you?"

"It's me," I said. "Mike O'Connor of 102 North Sylvia Street. I'm your friend."

"You're a Chinaman," he growled. "You're not Mike O'Connor."

I could only stutter a nonsensical reply.

"And who are these other Chinamen," said Zorro, pointing his dueling sword at Johnny, Terry, Billy, David, and Tass.

"We're Cub Scouts, Sir; Den 27, Mrs. O'Connor's Den. Don't kill us."

Then Zorro suddenly ripped off his mask, and there he was: our principal!

"Mr. Elmsworth!" we all gasped, and I woke up.

My poor mother took a while to recover from the international event. She always sought to show us in the best light, and persisted at it, but things relating to our den worked out less often than they worked out well. Mom had good ideas, but our execution of them went regularly haywire. I won't even mention the field trip when Tass Reynolds and Johnny Ratchet wandered away from the plant identification area and were lost in the woods for five hours, or the time my mother took us to Aberdeen to ride the train back to Montesano, and Billy Fitzgerald got off in Montesano with the rest of us, but when no one was looking, got back on the train and rode all the way to Olympia.

Most of the other dens seemed to function like little clocks, while our den—comprised of a lot of poor kids of loggers, mill workers, cascara gatherers, and pea pickers—didn't function that way. Because I had so many friends in the (how shall I say?) more professional dens, I sometimes thought of changing camps. But there was something realer ("lea-ler") about our den. For instance, when we studied woodcraft, who better to practice with than the kids who had excellent credentials in woodshed and stove craft, lacking as they did electric or oil heat?

When it came to building soapbox derby cars, birdhouses or forts, who knew better how to handle hammers, screwdrivers, and handsaws, or shoot birds for that matter? And further, who knew better than working-class kids how to fight, swear, and take a licking without crying? No, I had too much to learn from these kids, especially since my family had no woodshed, wood stove, handguns, and never swore (within earshot).

Sadly, it was my mother who had to run herd on our ragtag den. Having my mother as den mother had its disadvantages, but it also had an advantage. Mother being who she was didn't want to favor me over the other kids, the other urchins, so most of the time I had to restrain my strong leadership tendencies. I couldn't be as aggressive or so witty with my own mom being the den mother. But the advantage that I had over everyone was that the den meetings were held right in my own house, and once a meeting was over, I'd be exactly where I needed to be for a quick change out of my den shirt, den tie, and pants (what is known as one's good clothes) and into my baseball or football duds. This aspect of my life was so important—I mean getting quickly changed and out onto the fields of play—that I tried several times sleeping in my play clothes at night, even keeping my tennis shoes on. This was done on weekends and was my way of saving time dressing in the morning. The last time I tried this routine was after we had poured the cement for the Fort, and I was eager to get up early in the morning to go see how our new walkway had set up. I went outside and hurried over to the Fort and took a step *in* the concrete. It was supposed to be a step *on* the concrete. That somehow soured my taste for sleeping all night in my play clothes.

I didn't know anything concrete about where we got the concrete, which technically was cement that we were hoping—with a little luck—would become concrete. Jimmy Dockers was right; we should have placed an ad in the *Montesano Vidette,* reading:

Hey, please help! We have made a nearly concrete walkway, but the cement hasn't done what it was billed to do. It's okay to come to my father's property. He's doing highly critical work for the Department of Agriculture in Olympia all week. Just drop by. Don't mind the dog, Carolina; she is very old and only bites girls who hit her with sandbox shovels (that is she did it once). Will accept help; will talk to, and take candy from, strangers. Thank you very much. The Fort.

I think the adults in town were a little afraid of the Fort; I think they were a little afraid of us. I've noticed how parents are often stumped about what to do when their children do something that isn't in one of their recipe books for kid breeding and rearing. It's panic time. For example, I saw one of my cousins once walk in on a card game my parents and my aunts and uncles were engrossed in one evening; he was carrying my Uncle Jack's shotgun. I don't know if it was loaded, but as he toddled into the living room carrying it, going goo-goo, all the parents clearly demonstrated by their agitation that such a circumstance had never been outlined in their books for rearing.

I have to assume that there were mixed opinions regarding the Fort. "Men, I think we should help the children. Hard to believe, but we were, after all, kids once ourselves, a hundred years ago."

In a way, despite our making a big deal out of our Fort, it was a failure in some respects, even beyond the cement problem; a failure because we had enough wood to add several more stories, but because of the lean in it after three stories, we feared pushing our luck (we feared pushing the Fort). It had been my hope to build high enough to be able to see out past the back of my house to the tidal Chehalis River. We thought it would be terrific to watch the tugboats pulling the log booms down the river to the mills in Aberdeen. I also wanted the Fort high enough to run a tin can & string telephone line from the Fort to Paul Philips' big unpainted house across town. Little Johnny wanted it so high we could sit in the clouds (Little Johnny had trouble with his homework).

The lesson I did learn from all this unexpectedly was that very often when a kid has a dream, idea, or expectation, it's sometimes best to stop right there. That may be the best part. The dream realized, the idea followed through, or an expectation built up too strongly can easily lead to reality. And when I woke up that morning with my clothes already on and rushed out to the Fort to see the new concrete walkway, the reality was mud. But I should add that the universe can work in just the opposite way: the surprise birthday party; the big gift that wasn't under the Christmas tree but in the closet; the girl who hated you for pulling her hair and who has threatened to tell the teacher, but as she runs down the hall, trips and knocks herself out, and subsequently comes down with a case of amnesia.

But to return to the subplot (if anyone is still with me) and then to the main plot shortly: I'd sometimes hear Mom while she was having coffee with other moms trying to encourage them to take a turn heading up a den, our den.

"Mabel, you'd love working with them. You have such a way with kids, anyway."

"No thanks, Shirley, I can hardly keep my little Buddy's nose out of gas tanks every day, let alone keep track of a whole warren of Cub Scouts."

"Den."

"How's that?"

"I think you meant to say a whole *den* of cub scouts.

"Whatever."

Poor Mom. And later she just about had Mrs. Thomson convinced to take on the duties, but Mrs. Thompson, apparently wasn't going to be Mrs. Thompson much longer.

"I'd really love to Shirley, you know that, but Ed's leaving me. The timing isn't right."

Poor Mom. She was forced to stay on as Den Mother until the following year when our den dissolved due to most of us moving on, briefly, to Boy Scouts. (After learning how to tie fifty kinds of knots wrong and taken too many Scout oaths, I resigned my tenderfoot badge, convinced I could find in less structured pastimes more fun.)

But back to the main plot: Terry, Johnny, and I were loafing in the dry grass waiting for some of the other neighbor kids to arrive when I had a thought about China. "Hey, ever since you guys nearly dropped me on that stage at the library, I've been thinking about what Mrs. Whipple told us in geography. She said China is straight down below us on the other side of the globe.

"It's good they're down there," said Terry, "Because my dad doesn't like them."

"Does he know any of them?" I asked.

"Sure. At Camp Randall, where the loggers live, they got one for a cook."

"And your Dad doesn't like him?"

"He likes him okay. He's a good cook. But my dad says he would never invite him to our house."

"Well, maybe the cook wouldn't want to come to your house. It's not such a hot house, you know."

"What are you trying to say," said Terry, getting all red like his hair.

"I'm just saying it's strange that your dad likes the cook but won't invite him to your house. My dad doesn't like politicians from Olympia or Washington D.C., but he still invites them once in a while to dinner."

"I saw a Negro once," said the younger Ratchet.

"Well, big deal," said Jerry, still irritated. "I've seen three."

"I waved at one in Seattle once," I said.

The Negro I'd seen was driving a bread truck right along side of our two-door Ford as we drove southbound out of Seattle. I waved at him and he smiled and I waved even harder and he waved back. My mother seeing me do it, looked at the Negro and the Negro looked at her and laughed. My mother laughed too, then the bread truck sped away. My mother told my father and then he chuckled about it also. "That was a Negro wasn't it, Mom?"

"Yes, son."

Terry Rachet said, "I've seen three right here in Montesano. They don't live here, though; they live in the South."

"You mean Raymond?" I asked.

"No, further. Way south. Maybe Portland."

"Speaking of South. Real South. I've got a great idea. Let's dig to China."

"Dig to China?" said Jerry.

"China?" said Little Johnny.

"It's right under our feet, bigger than the state of Washington, just a long ways down, straight down."

It took some convincing, but Terry and Johnny went and got two shovels and came back to the yard. I tried to find a place not directly viewable from the windows at the back of the house so Dad wouldn't accidently spot us digging up his lawn. I found our pickaxe in our basement, but it was too heavy for any of us to swing, so I settled for a shovel from the tool shed.

It wasn't quite noon when we started digging, and within an hour we had a hole about three feet in diameter and two feet deep. That's when we began to hit old Chehalis River clay, and our progress slowed. By two o'clock we had a hole almost three feet deep, and though we hadn't run into hardpan yet, Terry and Johnny's enthusiasm was waning. But to my good fortune the two tardy neighbor kids, Leroy Simmons and Gary Short, arrived finally to play baseball, and were happy, however, to spell Terry and Little Johnny at the dig.

As we dug, I tried to imagine what we were going to say to the Chinamen when we popped up unannounced in their world. It would also be fun, I imagined, to bring back one or two for dinner in Montesano.

"What should we use," I'd ask my mother. "Chopsticks, or forks and knives?"

I also imagined the face on Mrs. Whipple in geography class, if I showed up with a Chinamen or a Chinese boy. "You're late for class, Mike," she might begin, but then catching sight of my pigtailed friend, she'd say, "And who do we have here?" All the students in class would be straining their necks to take in the newcomer. It would be better than when I brought to school a chipmonk I'd trapped in a Have-a-Heart trap baited with peanut butter.

"This is so-and-so from China. I found him, Mrs. Whipple, when I followed your directions and dug to China."

We worked on through the afternoon, but my strength was ebbing, just as enthusiasm was leaving the two late arrivals.

"And how far down did you say we have to dig?" asked Leroy.

"We should be getting close," I said.

"Are you sure the hole is in the right place?" asked Gary, who was tall though his surname was Short.

"That's one thing I'm absolutely sure of; China is bigger than the state of Washington; how could we miss it?"

"There's getting to be rock now and hardpan. I don't think we can dig any deeper unless we use dynamite," said Leroy.

"Dynamite?!" I said. That sounded interesting.

"I think I see a better way," I said. "Let's start a new hole over closer to the Fort. There's a good chance the digging will be easier." (I was dreaming now.)

"I don't want to," said Leroy. "I'm tired."

"Me too," said Gary. "I think it would be easier just to get on one of our rafts down in the South Monte swamps, push out into the Chehalis, and sail down to Aberdeen to be shanghaied."

"That shanghaiing stuff is from the old days. They don't do that sort of thing ever since they built a high school," I said.

"Well, listen, Mike," said Leroy. "Why don't you go down to the river and get on a raft and give it a try? I'm going home for supper," and he threw his shovel down.

"Yeah," said Gary. "I quit too," and he threw his shovel right on Leroy's shovel with an emphatic clang.

I could only sigh. And then that old empty sensation—like when a black cloud appears over the playfield—hit me. I looked into that dark hole, on which we had spent the labors of an afternoon, and, of course, it didn't look anything like China; it looked like Montesano.

27 CHILD LABORS

THE FIRST PAYING job I ever held was sweeping the parking lot of the Dairy Queen on Saturday mornings. The Dairy Queen was located at the west end of town just across Highway 101 from the Pentecostal Christian church, of which I had heard high-rollers made up the greatest share of the congregation (my sister informed me that they weren't *high-rollers* at all; they were *holy-rollers*). My pay at the Dairy Queen was a soft ice cream cone and a quarter. Customarily I favored a double-scoop, hard-ice cream cone, but because of my work at the Dairy Queen, I acquired a taste for soft-and-swirled despite its coming in only one flavor, and impersonally from a stainless-steel machine.

Paul Philips and I started a lawn-cutting business. I did better at it than any job of my Montesano commercial period. Paul had his dad's lawn mower and I had my dad's. To drum up business, Paul and I pushed the mowers around town looking for lawns with tall grass and dandelions that usually came with rundown houses. These lawns stood out easily from the rest, and upon locating one, we'd leave our mowers on the sidewalk and go up to the door of the house and knock. If a little old lady lived in the house, it could take awhile for her to answer the door. Mrs. Goldman kept calling from inside the house, "I'm coming, I'm coming," but she never came. Mrs. Goldman, my mother said, was ninety-two years old, older than Montesano, older than the fir tree in our yard!

Mrs. Howard, who lived only two blocks from our school, also was a little old lady (little old ladies came in two types: sweet or scary). We remembered her house because on Halloween we had waxed her windows believing nobody was home. I didn't expect her to be home this time because her small wooden house had a broken porch and the grass and weeds in her yard were as high as the crossbar on our makeshift goal posts. But we knocked anyway and Mrs. Howard answered so quickly we nearly fell off the broken porch in surprise.

"Boys," she said happily. "What can I help you with?" She looked a lot like my Olympia, non-farm grandmother.

"Hello, Mrs. Howard. Paul and I were wondering if you'd like your lawn cut. We're fast, trustworthy, and cheap."

"Oh, I'm sure you are all of that," she said. "Ed, my husband, you know, is still in the hospital for his back, so I've had to let go so much in the yard and house."

"We're very sorry," I said. "We only charge a dollar."

"Oh, please, don't worry about that. I'll gladly pay you *each* a dollar," Mrs. Howard said. "But don't cut your toes off."

Sometimes a prospective customer would be a stranger, maybe an unshaven, unemployed mill worker or logger in a ragged tee-shirt and old moccasins (a look not altogether different from that of Paul Philips' father, our chess master).

These folks often responded to our solicitations rudely, as if we kids were the source of their oppression. "What the hell do you want?" Ruder even than certain jailbirds we knew at the courthouse. If there was a woman in the house, we always preferred talking to her. "Hey, Harry, don't yell at them, they're just kids, for god's sake! They're only trying to turn a buck, which is more than you've been doing lately."

"Stuff it, Irma. I don't want a bunch of kids messing with the yard."

"What yard? I can't even see to the street anymore."

"I don't care. I don't want those kids in my yard."

Then Irma in her housecoat would say to us, "Boys, I'm sorry Hank's in such a bad mood. You'd better find someone else's yard to mow." And, "You boys are cute; do you know that? I bet you have lots of girlfriends."

With two lawn mowers churning through the tall grass and weeds, it never took us long to do a job. Our business ended, though, when my father pointed out to me that his lawn mower was wearing out, and did I have enough money saved to maintain it or buy another. (This I learned later was an example of the hidden-cost theory of not appreciating your machinery, or not capitalizing the word Equipment.)

Of course, both Paul and I had been throwing money around like it grew on lawns, which for us, it did. I liked to buy candy for my wood-heat friends; it was always a good feeling. My Olympia, non-farm grandmother, who often gave me a little money when she visited, always, though, warned me not to be a big shot. "Here's a few dollars from Grandfather and me, but don't be a big shot." Grandmother was right: buying my friends candy did make me feel like a big shot, which I liked and my friends seemed to like, too. The only bad thing I could figure out about being a big shot was when you didn't have the extra resources to be one, you remembered what it felt like being one before, and because that was before and this was after, you felt suddenly like a little shot; but I don't think real big shots are that introspective.

I wasn't stupid, though, about money. I always set aside quarters for beans and split peas for whenever a bean-shooting conflict might break out in a neighborhood. I bought a lot of small toys from Bullard's toy store, but since most of them were now made in Japan, they were inexpensive. The most expensive thing I bought was perfume for my mother on her birthday at the drugstore just across the street from the Bee Hive Koffee Shop. It cost eight whole dollars and because I didn't have quite that much, Ben Waxman, the druggist, let me put it on my mother's account.

One early enterprise of mine and my sister and fellow neighborhood entrepreneurs was selling candy bars in front of the steps to our house. We'd buy a discount pack of five Hersey Bars or Almond Joys, for instance, for the price of four, or 20 cents, at Mr. Pickering's grocery store, then try to sell five of them for a net profit of five cents. But business was very slow on our beloved maple-lined Sylvia Street, and we usually ate most of the merchandise ourselves.

We tried once to sell finger paintings on the street and old comic books, but the best we could do was a trade for the latter and a give-away for the former. Some people wouldn't even take (wouldn't even touch) our finger paintings when we offered them for free. ("You don't like that one. Here, let me whip you out something more suited to your taste. You can even sit there, on my wagon, while you wait.")

A more successful venture—and one I repeated—was collecting soda pop and beer bottles for the deposit money. Randy Hopkins and I actually collected the equivalent of five wagons full of bottles, and over two days, dragged each wagon load down to Mr. Pickering's grocery store. He didn't mind the first wagon, but by the third and fourth, he was becoming less patient as he had to count each bottle at the back of the store in the dimly lighted stock room while the rest of the store went unattended.

"Boys, Boys, you're doing good work with all this, and I'm happy to pay you the refund, but I'm short of help here, and you can see all the customers out front are waiting to be helped."

"Mr. Pickering, Sir. I think you missed that beer bottle."

Some kids by the fifth or sixth grades had paper routes for the *Aberdeen World,* but it was an evening paper and had to be delivered right after school. I wasn't about to hand over to the *Aberdeen World* any of my world of quality playtime.

The only other job I had in Montesano was a temporary one with Pete Baylor. It was a job for his dad, who owned the Western Auto Supply store. Mr. Baylor, who loved minor league baseball, said he'd give us a penny for every handbill we put on the porches of homes in town. This sounded like a much better deal than when my cousin Freddy and I were paid a penny for every chicken roost we cleaned on my Irish grandmother's farm.

The Western Auto job looked like the real deal, one that could put Pete and me on Easy Street, wherever that was; it could surely keep us in candy and sports gear for a season. Mr. Bauer had five hundred handbills printed. He insisted that we must not put more than one handbill on any one porch and, he emphasized, we absolutely must not toss any away.

"Do you understand?" He was looking more at me than at his son.

"Yes, Sir," I said, looking more up at the ceiling than at him. I was superstitious in those days; I didn't want to look at a gift horse.

We began our workday enthusiastically, covering downtown with alacrity because there weren't any porches, and then moving on to residential areas. One thing that slowed us was stopping to count how many handbills we had left and how much money we had made. Since we'd only got started, we hadn't made anything, but it was an obsession that was hard to curb, even after we realized we were spending more time counting handbills than distributing them.

By twelve strokes of the courthouse clock, however, we had passed out 120 handbills and made 60 cents each. It was going slower than we had expected, so we pushed on to other neighborhoods, up long walkways to big porches, through picket fence gates to little cottages, past barking dogs, black cats, through water sprinklers, past Billy Fletcher on his merry way to the Little Store, past moms with big-headed babies in strollers, past the postman, past Pete's classmate Carla Anderson, who stuck her tongue out at us, past Billy

Fletcher again returning from the Little Store with a fist full of red and black licorice sticks.

By four o'clock, Pete and I together had passed out 150 handbills, but still, in our arms, was the potential to distribute another 350. Tired, we pushed on past the five o'clock clanging of the courthouse bell as the reddening sun began melting in the western trees. That's when it hit me.

I was in the middle of a Russian saga!

Well, not exactly. I was in a story with the same theme as the one presented by Adolph Menjou on television called "How Much Land Does a Man Need?" which I later learned was adopted from the story of the same name by Leo Tolstoy, the land-owning Russian writer who often asked that question of himself.

The presentation on TV portrayed a peasant who had grown wealthy with land, but wanted more. He went to a far country where tribal people said they would give him some of their land if he participated in a contest of sorts. He was up for anything if he could just get his hands on more hectares. The peasant was told he could claim all the land that he could run around in one day, but he had to be back at the place—the top of a hill actually—where he had started from before five o'clock, or when the sun went down. I assumed the tribe didn't want the event to run past supper.

The wealthy peasant took off running at daybreak with a joyous surge of energy and everywhere he went, the land was good, and he couldn't believe that everywhere he went the land was his—or soon would be. When the scorching sun reached noon, he realized he'd better turn around so as to be sure to make it back by sunset, but he kept seeing more land that he wanted—a little knoll with a clear stream flowing below it; a stretch of ground where a copse of trees grew. He couldn't stop running.

The sun beat hotter and the peasant was wet with sweat and his sides ached, so finally, it got into him he had better turn back and, in fact, run like the dickens to make the deadline. Although the peasant was a greedy one, you had to root for him.

He fell down every so often because, while he was still running hard, his legs were weakening. This added to the gathering drama. He had to get back or all the land he had staked out for himself that day would remain with the tribe. He was covering a lot of ground and it looked as though he might just make it, but then the sun went down in the west and it appeared he wouldn't make it, but then he saw the tribesmen on the hill in the east where he had started from, and they were still standing in sunlight, so it looked as if he might make it after all, and he ran up the little last hill and fell at the feet of the tall chieftain, who was standing somberly erect, his spear still reflecting light, and he'd made it! But, oh no, he was dead!

With the sun now almost vanished in the colored clouds, Pete and I rushed on with all our strength to distribute the handbills. I came to a grate over a sewer drain. The load of handbills in my pack was still heavy, in fact, it felt heavier. I called to Pete. He came over sweaty and tired. "Look here," I said, pointing at the grated cavity.

"How about we put a few handbills in there? Just to lighten the load. If we can lighten the load, it will mean we can actually pass out more handbills than if we carry what we have," I reasoned.

"I don't know if we should," said Pete, the boss's son.

"Well, maybe we should just go home, then."

"What about hiding just a dozen or so in there?" said Pete.

"Sure," I said. "That's fair."

We slipped a dozen or so into the drain and moved on. Then we realized we were back in a neighborhood not far from the courthouse that we had already covered.

"I'm getting real hungry," said Pete.

"Me too," I said. "But I think your dad won't be happy if we bring back any handbills. Let's find some place to put a few more."

"I guess so," said Pete.

It became easier and easier to rationalize ditching handbills. "There's no point in keeping them, when you think about it," I said. "Tomorrow's the sale; what good will they be then?"

"I suppose you're right," said Pete.

It took too much time to find perfect hiding places for the handbills, so we just started dropping some on lawns and scattering others in the street. We began doing this with one handbill at a time, but soon were "distributing" them by the handfuls. Our fatigue and hunger made us rather giddy, and toward the end of our adventure, we were throwing handbills into the air like confetti in the middle of the street. We weren't painting the town; we were papering it!

The next day, Western Auto Supply had one of its most successful sales. Pete's father was naturally pleased with how it went, and paid us two and a half dollars each. It was only later when the Better Business Bureau received numerous complaints about having handbills thrown all over local yards that Mr. Baylor, who also coached our Little League Baseball team, Vancouver Door (we went 7-3 that season), threatened to bench us for the next game. To play in the next game was worth far more than the two and a half dollars.

But Mr. Baylor actually had no intention of benching us that game (he wasn't so small minded and he needed Pete at first base and me at second since we had only ten players, including two pitchers). And he also let us keep our wages. Considering there were only some 2,000 people in Montesano, distributing 500 handbills properly was rather impossible if you think about it.

28 LEAVING MONTESANO

EVEN A WHOLE year before it, my parents were prepping my sister and me for the move from Montesano. It was a government transfer for my dad to either Everett, Auburn, or Port Angeles. Knowing how rooted I was in Montesano, my parents were wise to give me a year's notice; it allowed me time to step into the role of the kid who was leaving town. *Sayonara.*

I knew there had been talk of partitioning my sister's and my long attic bedroom; I slept on the north side and my sister on the south, and the brick chimney that came up from our fireplace in the living room through my side of the room on its way to the roof, made a warm, partial wall behind which I slept, and gave my sister the privacy that Mom and Dad wanted to enhance with a partition. I guess my sister, three years older than I, was officially now a teenager, but to me it seemed that dividing the room would make her space smaller, more cramped. I just assumed she wanted teen privacy for the same inscrutable reasons her part of the long room looked so different from mine. In fact, I was forbidden to go into her side of the room (it held her marching baton, dolls, Nancy Drew mysteries, a mirror, and a dresser with a ruffled gingham dresser stool).

True, when I was very little, my sister would invite me to sit on her bed while she read to me. Even then she knew she was going to be a schoolteacher. One day, in one of the books, I recognized my first printed word, "is." A whole lot of words have come after that one (obviously), but because it was the first word in a book I recognized and pronounced, I can still see it vividly on that page. In the legends of my youth, the moment must qualify as my toehold on literacy, my first step out of the swamps and duckweed along the Chehalis River of South Monte.

"Is," I said, pointing to the word and looking wide eyed up at my sister.

"Is," she said.

"Is," I said again.

"Yes, good," my sister said. "Now, let me finish the story."

As I was saying, I didn't go into her room uninvited to look at anything there (I did once or twice and that was enough) because her things were as different from mine as musicals from monster movies. (I won't digress to tell you how much I hated musicals. I still have nightmares from something called "Pajama Game." The story went along tolerably enough, but then everybody starts singing real corny songs, and in that particular musical, they were singing in their pajamas! I once got taken to "Damn Yankees," another musical, if you can call that music, and I had thought the motion picture was going to be about either the Civil War or baseball. I don't remember what it turned out to be about, but it had all the same corny talk-more-than-sing songs breaking up the story line just like in "Pajama Game." Adult popular culture, I felt, was quite immature.)

My room, in contrast to my sister's—just to give you a few de-tails—had yellow wallpaper with cowboys and cowpunchers on it. I had a small desk where I actually did homework once to learn the multiplication tables, with some help from my sister, because the teacher had said it was time we started learning them, and learn-ing too, what homework was. Homework was what you put off doing until the last minute, but worried you all the time before you did it.

I kept my sports equipment on or under the desk most of the time. In one corner of my room I had a box of marbles (many of the marbles had names and personalities), a smaller box of base-ball cards, miniature tin license plates of all the states, Korean War cards, and my sacred stack of autographed pictures of the Notre Dame football team. (I had written the team to tell them how much I liked them, and that I was going to play for them when I grew up, and I was really Irish too, because my father was born in County Cork, and he would have been President except for the fine print of the Constitution.)

I had a small bookcase with mostly Dr. Doolittle books, school readers, and Hardy Boys mysteries, and against one wall, my stack of games including Uncle Rich, Mr. Ree, Monopoly, Clue, photo-electric football, ping-pong basketball, Uncle Wiggley, Easy Money, chess, Pit, etc. I don't recall where I kept my clothes, maybe down-stairs in the piano room. My bed was built into the wall, a bed you couldn't climb under or move, which eliminated any need I might have to retrieve errant marbles from dark and cobwebby corners, and any fears I might have of snakes or ghosts under there.

Mostly I remember the window above the bed (oh, and that warmth the chimney gave off) with the view into our big back yard. I'm not exaggerating when I say when I woke up and heard the rob-ins singing in the fir and maple trees, under the light cover of gray clouds, and looked out the window at the great Fort standing tall (and crooked) unpainted in pale light, my heart leaped like a trout breaking water on Lake Sylvia. Those noisy robins were a cheerful chorus most mornings from spring through windy autumn (the first days of autumn anyway), and I always missed them in the dark of winter when my thoughtful mother would leave a small light burn-ing at the top of the stairs.

That window was convenient, too, because if I had to pee in the night, I could do it right out it while standing on my bed looking up at the stars. My father, the agriculture expert, found me out because the grass below the window stayed green and lush when the rest of his carefully cultivated lawn withered for the year. I was only lightly scolded for this, and it later became a source of some amusement for my parents' friends when Mom or Dad told how the grass was greener on my side of the house.

I learned over time that if I did something that wasn't too heinous and that had a humorous angle to it, my parents might scold me, but behind the bluster of the scolding they could actually be getting a little kick out of whatever I was being scolded for. I might be stumbling into some darker psychology here than I really want to. I think it comes back to an example: When your dog is a puppy and he or she does something goofy like chews up a book a neighbor lent to your parents everyone is horrified, and breaking the news to the neighbor who owned the book is handled very seriously and apologetically. "I'm so sorry, Doris. Here's back your abridged *Decline and Fall of the Roman Empire*. Puppy Filbert abridged it further."

But later, when the parents are having coffee and the neighbor in question isn't there, the whole incident retold makes for a good laugh. "And when I handed back to her that book with the teeth marks all over the cover and torn pages hanging out from the chapter on Christian zealots, I thought she was going to pass out. Puppy Filbert is just too naughty for his own good. Ha, ha, ha."

Roughly, that's how my parents took, I think, the discovery that I was watering Dad's lawn from great evening heights.

When the talk of moving began, it didn't, as I say, take me long to get used to the idea. The first day of my sixth grade year, I even informed my new teacher that I wouldn't be staying too long, feeling somehow that this announcement might win me some vaguely special status, a status that would immunize me from those report card denunciations, namely the one that followed me through every grade of school like a tail follows a monkey: UNNECESSARY TALKING. But my parents had already talked to the teacher (or Montesano being such small town, other people had told her who had heard it from my parents, or got it second or third hand from [who knows?] the Bee Hive Koffee Shop maybe, the milkman, the *Montesano Vidette?*) And the teacher said to me that, yes, I was going to move but not during the school year, not during her watch.

In fact, we didn't move until the following fall, and chose Port Angeles, a seaport town with a courthouse in Spanish style—like our firehouse and library—on the Straits of Juan de Fuca, in the lee of the Olympic Mountains, rather than Everett with its polluting mills or Auburn with its awful traffic where, my father said, was the most fertile farmland in the Northwest, now being paved over for Boeing space ship factories and business parks where no kids played or sang (though Auburn did have many used car lots with thousands of little flags and a spectacular view of our local volcano, Mount Rainier, the same name as a beer, a street, and a minor league baseball team).

It was on a Saturday in early September when we finally left for Port Angeles. I had gone to play football at the county field by the courthouse where the jail had windows from which incarcerated sports fans often looked out upon our play. I must have been growing up in some unconscious effortless way, just like my sister was doing, because when our Ford with my parents and sister and Carolina, our dog, drove up and parked along the curb at the field to fetch me, I just passed the ball to Jimmy Dockers and said with total cool and composure, goodbye, and then waved goodbye to my other friends. You'd have thought I was only going downtown to get a haircut from Roy Rogers, or going with my mother to Aberdeen to watch my sister dance in a recital with dozens of other girls, all tapping their brains out as if the floor was alive with spiders.

I got in the back seat of the car and rode with my parents past the courthouse. I looked back though the elliptical rear window and Jimmy was running like crazy down the sideline. For a moment, I thought he was running after our car, which put a big lump in my throat, but no, he was running for the end zone; he was scoring a touchdown. The game was going on just like before, without me. And my team, my former team, to be precise, was now behind a touchdown! It would have been time for me to call for a Flying Wedge on the kickoff, or a reverse in the shadows of the end zone pines. It would have been time to step up!

The car went around the lane by the courthouse and down the gentle hill to town and the main highway. We passed right through the heart of Montesano under the one stoplight with the Bee Hive Koffee Shop on the right and the drug store and brick hotel on the left. In no time we were driving past Safeway, the Mecury-Ford dealership and out past the sign that read Thanks for Visiting Montesano (pop. 2,431)—soon to be subtracted by four.

Then we were on the straight road heading east at 35 mph between the tall poplars, a stately row on each side of the highway. The small poplar leaves, turning color now with fall, fluttered in the blue sky where only a few white clouds were drifting slowly over the green hills. The gold leaves were delicately shimmering in a way I and no one else just then, I thought, could feel.

Soon we were out from between trees and heading due east at 50 mph toward Brady, with Satsop and Elma just beyond. Looking back through the rear window, I could only imagine I could still see the courthouse clock, the town, or anyone in it, or anything of it. The poplars were getting smaller and smaller as we drove east, until, at last, they were erased from view as chalk from a blackboard. I was getting a little carsick from facing the other direction than the car was going, so I turned around and looked ahead.

THE END

BOOKS FROM PLEASURE BOAT STUDIO: A LITERARY PRESS

(Note: Caravel Books is a new imprint of Pleasure Boat Studio: A Literary Press. Caravel Books is the imprint for mysteries only. Aequitas Books is another imprint which includes non-fiction with philosophical and sociological themes. Empty Bowl Press is a Division of Pleasure Boat Studio.)

God Is a Tree, and Other Middle-Age Prayers ~ Esther Cohen ~ $10

Home & Away: The Old Town Poems ~ Kevin Miller ~ $15

Old Tale Road ~ Andrew Schelling ~ an empty bowl book ~ $15

The Shadow in the Water ~ Inger Frimansson, trans. fm. Swedish by Laura Wideburg ~ a caravel mystery ~ $18

Working the Woods, Working the Sea ~ eds. Finn Wilcox and Jerry Gorsline ~ an empty bowl book ~ $22

Listening to the Rhino ~ Dr. Janet Dallett ~ an aequitas book ~ $16

The Woman Who Wrote King Lear, and Other Stories ~ Louis Phillips ~ $16

Weinstock Among the Dying ~ Michael Blumenthal ~ $18

The War Journal of Lila Ann Smith ~ Irving Warner ~ $18

Dream of the Dragon Pool: A Daoist Quest ~ Albert A. Dalia ~ $18

Good Night, My Darling ~ Inger Frimansson, Trans by Laura Wideburg ~ $18 ~ a caravel mystery

Falling Awake: An American Woman Gets a Grip on the Whole Changing World — One Essay at a Time ~ Mary Lou Sanelli ~ $15 ~ an aequitas book

Way Out There: Lyrical Essays ~ Michael Daley ~ $16 ~ an aequitas book

The Case of Emily V. ~ Keith Oatley ~ $18 ~ a caravel mystery

Monique ~ Luisa Coelho, Trans fm Portuguese by Maria do Carmo de Vasconcelos and Dolores DeLuise ~ $14

The Blossoms Are Ghosts at the Wedding ~ Tom Jay ~ $15 ~ an empty bowl book

Against Romance ~ Michael Blumenthal ~ poetry ~ $14

Speak to the Mountain: The Tommie Waites Story ~ Dr. Bessie Blake ~ $18 / $26 ~ an aequitas book

Artrage ~ Everett Aison ~ $15

Days We Would Rather Know ~ Michael Blumenthal ~ $14

Puget Sound: 15 Stories ~ C. C. Long ~ $14

Homicide My Own ~ Anne Argula ~ $16

Craving Water ~ Mary Lou Sanelli ~ $15

When the Tiger Weeps ~ Mike O'Connor ~ $15

Wagner, Descending: The Wrath of the Salmon Queen ~ Irving Warner ~ $16

Concentricity ~ Sheila E. Murphy ~ $13.95

Schilling, from a study in lost time ~ Terrell Guillory ~ $16.95

Rumours: A Memoir of a British POW in WWII ~ Chas Mayhead ~ $16

The Immigrant's Table ~ Mary Lou Sanelli ~ $13.95

The Enduring Vision of Norman Mailer ~ Dr. Barry H. Leeds ~ $18

Women in the Garden ~ Mary Lou Sanelli ~ $13.95

Pronoun Music ~ Richard Cohen ~ $16

If You Were With Me Everything Would Be All Right ~ Ken Harvey ~ $16

The 8th Day of the Week ~ Al Kessler ~ $16

Another Life, and Other Stories ~ Edwin Weihe ~ $16

Saying the Necessary ~ Edward Harkness ~ $14

Nature Lovers ~ Charles Potts ~ $10

In Memory of Hawks, & Other Stories from Alaska ~ Irving Warner ~ $15

The Politics of My Heart ~ William Slaughter ~ $12.95

The Rape Poems ~ Frances Driscoll ~ $12.95

When History Enters the House: Essays from Central Europe ~ Michael Blumenthal ~ $15

Setting Out: The Education of Lili ~ Tung Nien ~ Trans fm Chinese by Mike O'Connor ~ $15

Our Chapbook Series:

No. 1: The Handful of Seeds: Three and a Half Essays - Andrew Schelling - $7

No. 2: Original Sin - Michael Daley - $8

No. 3: Too Small to Hold You - Kate Reavey - $8

No. 4: The Light on Our Faces: A Therapy Dialogue - Lee Miriam Whitman Raymond - $8

No. 5: Eye - William Bridges - $8

No. 6: Selected New Poems of Rainer Maria Rilke - Trans fm German by Alice Derry - $10

No. 7: Through High Still Air: A Season at Sourdough Mountain - Tim McNulty - $9

No. 8: Sight Progress - Zhang Er, Trans fm Chinese by Rachel Levitsky - $9

No. 9: The Perfect Hour - Blas Falconer - $9

No. 10: Fervor - Zaedryn Meade - $10

From other publishers (in limited editions):

Desire - Jody Aliesan - $14 (an Empty Bowl book)

Deams of the Hand - Susan Goldwitz - $14 (an Empty Bowl book)

Lineage - Mary Lou Sanelli - $14 (an Empty Bowl book)

The Basin: Life in a Chinese Province - Mike O'Connor - $10 (an Empty Bowl book)

The Straits - Michael Daley - $10 (an Empty Bowl book)

In Our Hearts and Minds: The Northwest and Central America - Ed. Michael Daley - $12 (an Empty Bowl book)

The Rainshadow - Mike O'Connor - $16 (an Empty Bowl book)

Untold Stories - William Slaughter - $10 (an Empty Bowl book)

In Blue Mountain Dusk - Tim McNulty - $12.95 (a Broken Moon book)

China Basin - Clemens Starck - $13.95 (a Story Line Press book)

Journeyman's Wages - Clemens Starck - $10.95 (a Story Line Press book)

Orders: Pleasure Boat Studio

books are available by order from your bookstore, directly from PBS, or through the following:

SPD (Small Press Distribution)
Tel. 800.869.7553, Fax 5105240852

Partners/West Tel. 425.227.8486,
Fax 425.204.2448

Baker & Taylor 800.775.1100,
Fax 800.775.7480

Ingram Tel 615.793.5000, Fax 615.287.5429

Amazon.com or Barnesandnoble.com

How we got our name

…from "Pleasure Boat Studio," an essay written by Ouyang Xiu, Song Dynasty poet, essayist, and scholar, on the twelfth day of the twelfth month in the *renwu* year (January 25, 1043):

> "I have heard of men of antiquity who fled from the world to distant rivers and lakes and refused to their dying day to return. They must have found some source of pleasure there. If one is not anxious for profit, even at the risk of danger, or is not convicted of a crime and forced to embark; rather, if one has a favorable breeze and gentle seas and is able to rest comfortably on a pillow and mat, sailing several hundred miles in a single day, then is boat travel not enjoyable? Of course, I have no time for such diversions. But since 'pleasure boat' is the designation of boats used for such pastimes, I have now adopted it as the name of my studio. Is there anything wrong with that?"

Translated by Ronald Egan

GREEN PRESS INITIATIVE